BENY

PATRICK
VAN
ROSENDAAL

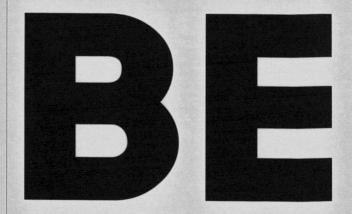

BE

FROM TOURIST TO NEW YORKER
WITH PATRICK VAN ROSENDAAL

LANNOO

NY

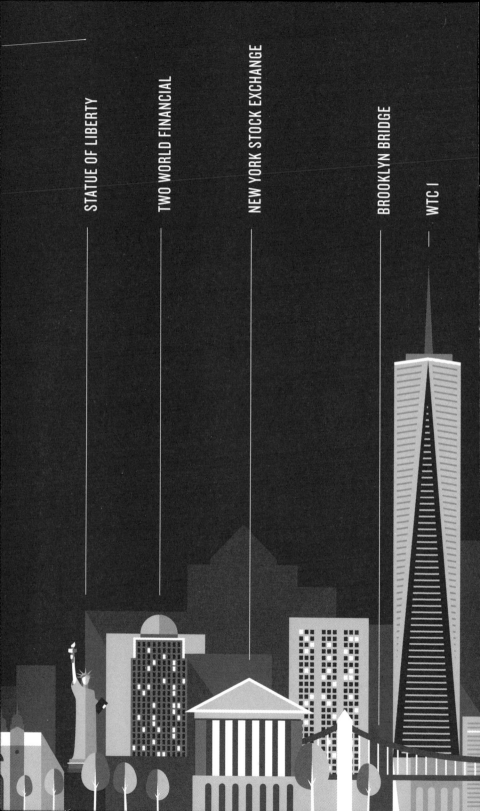

STATUE OF LIBERTY

TWO WORLD FINANCIAL

NEW YORK STOCK EXCHANGE

BROOKLYN BRIDGE

WTC I

WOOLWORTH BUILDING

EMPIRE STATE BUILDING

CHRYSLER BUILDING

NEW YORK ICONS

Who is Patrick van Rosendaal?

A FEW TIPS FROM PATRICK

On your journey through this book and around the city, Patrick is with you, providing tips that will make your visit to New York smoother and more pleasant.

ADDRESSES

Patrick embarked on his sales and marketing career in Paris at the end of the 1990s. He is an alumnus of the prestigious Vlerick Business School and had already seen a great deal of the world before finally settling in New York. Having previously lived in Paris and London, he was no stranger to life in a huge metropolis. But then his life took an unexpected turn of events. Patrick followed his heart to the United States, only to lose it in New York. He exchanged his wedding ring for true love and nestled in Lady Liberty's lap. A lady with plentiful potential and mesmerizing magnetism, as well as a feisty female who is no pushover.

As with every good relationship, it was a story of ups and downs. A story of financial lows and business highs; of decadent excesses and serene introspection; of living and surviving; of frequent fighting and occasional giving up. But always the story was extraordinarily fascinating and at breakneck speed.

In particular, it was a story about people. On his travels, Patrick met countless New Yorkers who helped mold his life. Colorful characters, each with their own personality and unique perspective on life, but all with one thing in common: all of them love the same amazing city. This gave him a peek at real New York life. It didn't take long for the spell to be cast, causing Patrick's attraction to New York to evolve into pure passion. The urge to share it with his fellow Belgians made him decide to become a professional tour guide. He passed the official examination and started working for the well-known New York Gray Line busses and for Bike and Roll, the leading company for guided bike tours. Since then, his career as a tour guide has skyrocketed.

Since becoming an official member of GANYC, the prestigious association for professional tour guides, he has gone through three scooters and many a pair of shoes over his thousands of miles of city exploration. And his city tour guide company, BE NY, has become increasingly successful. Patrick and his team have given more than 15,000 visitors an unforgettable experience. Therefore, in his own words, he has been blessed with the world's best job.

TABLE OF CONTENTS

WALKING TOUR WALKING TOUR WALKING TOUR

1 2 3

COME AS A TRAVELER, GO AS A NEW YORKER
Midtown
Manhattan
12 - 21

EVOLVING NEW YORK
The Villages
46 - 55

FROM YUPPIE TO HIPSTER
Downtown FiDi
to Williamsburg
82 - 93

Getting around in New York

GEOGRAPHY

When you think of New York, you often think Manhattan skyscrapers. But this city is obviously so much more than that. New York is an agglomeration of five large areas, or *boroughs*: Manhattan, The Bronx in the north, Queens in the east, Brooklyn in the southeast and, finally, Staten Island in the south.

Each of these boroughs has its very own neighborhoods; Manhattan's being the most famous of all. Their names generally have an ethnic or geographical origin. The former would include Chinatown, Koreatown and Little Italy. The latter has spawned such names as Upper East Side, Upper West Side, the West Village, Lower East Side, SoHo (South of Houston), NoHo (North of Houston), TriBeCa (Triangle Below Canal Street), NoLIta (North of Little Italy), FiDi (Financial District), DUMBO (Down Under Manhattan and Brooklyn Bridge Overpass), and so on.

Officially, New York has 8.4 million inhabitants. But if you include all the businesspeople, tourists, and illegal immigrants, you could easily increase that figure by about 50%.

ORIENTATION

Manhattan, with the exception of Lower Manhattan, is crisscrossed by its well-known grid of streets and avenues. That makes finding your way a piece of cake. Follow these guidelines and you'll have a hard time getting lost:

FUN FACT
How did the boroughs get their names?

Manhattan comes from the Algonquin Lenape Indians, the native inhabitants of the island. They called Manhattan "Manahatta", which means something like hilly island.

Queens was one of the twelve New York counties under British rule and owes its name to Queen Catherine of Braganza, wife of King Charles II of England.

Brooklyn is derived from Breukelen, a town in the Netherlands. It is a reminder of the time when New York was still under Dutch rule, when its name was still New Amsterdam.

The same goes for Staten Island Staaten Eylandt was a Dutch trading post and refers to the Staten-Generaal (the States-General), the Dutch parliament.

The Bronx is named after the Swede Jonas Bronck, the European pioneer who settled there and who amassed a considerable amount of land.

- Avenues run from north to south. Streets from east to west.
- If you're heading north they call that Uptown, if you're heading south it's Downtown.
- 5th Avenue divides Manhattan into east and west. When you see the letters E or W in front of a street name (for example, E 50th Street) that tells you on which side of 5th Avenue your destination is located.
- The majority of streets are one-way; even-numbered streets run eastwards. So by looking at the traffic you can tell in which direction to head.
- The distance between streets is usually around 260 ft. The distance between avenues is about three or four times that.
- New Yorkers count in blocks, so addresses are specified by them. For example, "56th Street between 5th and 6th".

HOW DO YOU TRAVEL?

The predominant form of travel in New York is walking. 10 miles a day is not exceptional. For longer distances, take the subway, but if you're looking to get from A to B in comfort, you could always take a cab. Only a nut would actually try to explore Manhattan in a rental car. There's a general map of New York and its many neighborhoods on the inside cover.

A TRIP FROM PATRICK

Watch out for the avenues in the Midtown and Upper Manhattan region. Avenues are numbered from east to west and from 1 to 12 but, in a large area of Manhattan, after 1st, 2nd, and 3rd you get Lexington, Madison, and Park Avenue and only then, 5th, 6th, 7th, etc.

WALKING TOUR

COME AS A TRAVELER, GO AS A NEW YORKER
MIDTOWN MANHATTAN

COME AS A TRAVELER, GO AS A NEW YORKER

MIDTOWN MANHATTAN

🕐 **3 TO 4 HOURS**

1. GRAND CENTRAL TERMINAL
2. CHRYSLER BUILDING
3. NEW YORK PUBLIC LIBRARY
4. BRYANT PARK
5. TOURNEAU
6. FASHION WALK OF FAME - DIANE VON FURSTENBERG
7. HARD ROCK CAFE
8. THE LION KING
9. DISNEY STORE
10. SARDI'S RESTAURANT & GRILL
11. TKTS TIMES SQUARE
12. M&M'S WORLD
13. CARNEGIE HALL
14. BROADWAY COMEDY CLUB
15. THE PLAZA
16. WILLIAM TECUMSEH SHERMAN NATIONAL MONUMENT
17. BARNEY'S NEW YORK
18. APPLE FLAGSHIP STORE
19. NIKETOWN
20. TIFFANY & CO.
21. TRUMP TOWER
22. POLO RALPH LAUREN
23. MOMA
24. UNIQLO
25. ST. PATRICK'S CATHEDRAL
26. TOP OF THE ROCK
27. AMERICAN GIRL
28. INTERNATIONAL GEM TOWER
29. BARNES & NOBLE
30. NBA STORE

Just landed in the coolest city on earth? Then this is the tour for you. This walk starts at the magnificent Grand Central Terminal and then takes you, via 42nd Street, to the most prominent hotspots in central Manhattan. Feast your eyes on the impressive Empire State Building, the elegant Chrysler Building, and the dazzling library. Via charming Bryant Park you will arrive at the world-famous "Crossroads of the World," Times Square. Prepare to be overwhelmed by the flashing billboards, while the city's largest toy store will make your mouth water. You can also have your picture taken with the Naked Cowboy, discover where Frank Sinatra once had the shivers, and cross New York's busiest intersection where, deep below ground, more than 60 million passengers are in transit. The tour then takes you to Central Park and, finally, past renowned establishments such as Carnegie Hall and The Plaza Hotel, brings you to Fifth Avenue, New York's number one shopping street. This is a shopper's paradise. Ready (your credit card), set, go shopping!

① GRAND CENTRAL TERMINAL

Park Ave. and 42nd St.
www.grandcentralterminal.com
The best word to describe this historic monument, which handles 750,000 travelers daily, is 'majestic'. Next to the entrance to the Oyster Bar is the Whispering Corner. Why not give it a whisper?

② CHRYSLER BUILDING

405 Lexington Ave.
This sublime specimen of Art Deco was once the tallest building in New York *and* in the world. However, it lost the title in 1931 to the Empire State Building. But it still has a claim to fame: it's the tallest building on earth entirely constructed from bricks (though supported by a steel frame).

③ NEW YORK PUBLIC LIBRARY

5th Ave. and 42nd St.
www.nypl.org
🕐 Mo. 10 a.m.-6 p.m., Tu.-We. 10 a.m.-8 p.m., Th.-Sa. 10 a.m.-6 p.m., Su. 1 p.m.-5 p.m.
530,000 cubic feet of marble from all over the world were used to embellish the library. The Rose Main Reading Room is awe – inspiring and worth braving the stairs – at least for playing out the scene where Carrie Bradshaw from *Sex and the City* is stood up at the altar.

④ BRYANT PARK

Between 40th and 42nd St. and 5th and 6th Ave.
www.bryantpark.org
🕐 Oct. - Apr. 7 a.m.-10 p.m., May 7 a.m.-11 p.m., June - Sep. Mo.-Fr. 7 a.m.-midnight, Sa.-Su. 7 a.m.-11 p.m.
This beautifully maintained park, with its free Wi-Fi access and charging stations is perfect for internet addicts. Old school adherents will find *pétanque* courts, ping-pong tables, movies in the summer, a skating rink in the winter and more.

⑤ TOURNEAU

1095 6th Avenue, Manhattan
www.tourneau.com
🕐 Mo.-We. 9 a.m.-7 p.m., Th. 9 a.m.-8 p.m., Fr.-Sa. 9 a.m.-7 p.m., Su. 11 a.m.-6 p.m.
Leave as a New Yorker, that's the plan, right? If you want to completely blend in and lose the *tourist look* it may not be such a bad idea to drop by this watch store. Get a Rolex; after all you're in the business district.

⑥ FASHION WALK OF FAME – DIANE VON FURSTENBERG

7th Ave., between 39th and 40th St.

More than justified. The Belgian-American Diane von Furstenberg is deservedly immortalized here as one of the most successful fashion designers of all time.

⑦ HARD ROCK CAFE

1501 Broadway, Times Square
www.hardrock.com/cafes/new-york
🕐 Restaurant: Mo.-Su. 11 a.m.-1 a.m., breakfast: Sa.-Su. 8 a.m.-10 a.m.
🕐 Shop: daily 9 a.m.-1 a.m.

The best address for a somewhat overpriced hamburger of mediocre quality. Historically interesting as the former Paramount Theater where stars such as Frank Sinatra made their stage debut.

⑧ THE LION KING

200 West, 45th St., Times Square
www.lionking.com
🕐 Varying hours. Shows usually at 2 p.m. and 8 p.m.

This major Broadway classic is in its 20th year. The show is approaching its 7,000th performance to audiences of 1,500 per day.

⑨ DISNEY STORE

1540 Broadway, Manhattan
www.disneystore.com
🕐 Mo.-Su. 9 a.m.-1 a.m.

If you're still embittered by the disappearance of the world's most notorious red light district, you'd be advised to avoid this place – that's because it was the Walt Disney Company that was asked to make Times Square family-friendly again. Its success won it this prime location. Each day the very first guest is given the key to turn on the magic in an official ceremony.

⑩ SARDI'S RESTAURANT & GRILL

234 West, 44th St.
www.sardis.com
🕐 Tu.-Su. 12 p.m.-11:30 p.m.

Sardi's is an icon in the showbiz world. In exchange for a daily meal, Alex Gard started drawing caricatures of celebrities in the 1920s. Roughly 1,300 now adorn the walls.

⑪ TKTS TIMES SQUARE

Father Duffy Square, Times Square
www.tdf.org
🕐 Evening shows: Mo. We.-Sa. 3 p.m.-8 p.m., Tu. 2 p.m.-8 p.m., Su. 3 p.m.-7 p.m.
🕐 Afternoon shows: We., Th., Sa. 10 a.m.-2 p.m., Su. 11 a.m.-3 p.m.

If you can't manage to get to the Broadway show's own box office, then TKTS is your best bet. Since you can get discounts there of up to 50%, you'll obviously be the only one in line..... Get ready to shuffle.

⑫ M&M'S WORLD

1600 Broadway, between 48th and 49th St.
www.mmsworld.com
🕐 Mo.-Su. 9 a.m.- midnight

M&M's World greets you with a gigantic wall of "Mars & Murrie's." New York's largest candy store is a multicolored temptation.

⑬ CARNEGIE HALL

881 7th Ave.
www.carnegiehall.org
🕐 Varying hours depending on the show.

This world famous concert hall has divine acoustics. It opened in 1891, with Tchaikovsky as its very first conductor. Since the acoustics are specifically designed for music-making, cough drops are included in the price. How do you get in to Carnegie Hall? Practice, practice, practice. Buying a ticket also works.

⑭ BROADWAY COMEDY CLUB

318 W 53rd St.
www.broadwaycomedyclub.com
🕐 Mo.-Su. opens at 3 p.m.

The place where comedy is taken very seriously.

⑮ THE PLAZA

Plaza Hotel, 59th St. and 5th Ave.
www.theplazany.com

In bygone days, everybody who was anybody made an appearance at this luxurious hotel with a fabulous interior. It was built in 1907 for $12 million and sold to Donald Trump for thirty times as much. At a certain point he dumped it, together with his wife Ivana (who was also the hotel's manager). Today it's worth about $800 million. Over the years, the hotel has also served as a set for a whole slew of films, such as *Crocodile Dundee*, *Sleepless in Seattle* and, most recently, *The Great Gatsby*.

⑯ WILLIAM TECUMSEH SHERMAN MONUMENT

764 Doris C Freedman Place, Manhattan
www.centralparknyc.org/things-to-see-and-do/
attractions/william-tecumseh-sherman
🕐 Mo.-Su. 6 a.m.-1 a.m.

New York is a magnet for the sport freaks and this is the gateway to the world's largest gym. From here you can embark on a 6-mile tour through the most beautiful park in the world and, while you're at it, try not to be tempted by the countless burger, hotdog, and churro stands. *Ready? Set. Go!*

⑰ BARNEY'S NEW YORK

650 Madison Ave.
www.barneys.com
🕐 Mo.-Fr. 10 a.m.-8 p.m.,
Sa. 10 a.m.-7 p.m., Su. 11 a.m.-6 p.m.

The address for a dose of upper-class shopping.

Nine stories of exclusive and high-end collections. Their branches in Lower Manhattan and on the Upper West Side are also perfect for testing the limits of your credit card.

⑱ APPLE FLAGSHIP STORE

767 5th Ave. and 59th St.
www.apple.com/retail/fifthavenue
🕐 Daily, 24 hours

Enter the glass cube for the latest Mac or iPhone. Wi-Fi is free. Great for making everyone jealous on Foursquare, Facebook or Instagram. Open 24/7/365.

⑲ NIKETOWN

6 E 57th St.
store.nike.com
🕐 Mo.-Sa. 10 a.m.- 8 p.m.,
Su. 11 a.m.- 7 p.m.

Welcome to the sports fanatic's mecca! No fewer than five stories full! Since the Nike Air Max revival, also an interesting spot for hipsters and homesick trailer trash.

⑳ TIFFANY & CO.

727 5th Ave.
www.tiffany.com
🕐 Mo.-Sa. 10 a.m.-7 p.m.,
Su. 12 noon-6 p.m.

If you want to follow in Audrey Hepburn's footsteps, then it's time for breakfast here. And don't

forget your sunglasses. You don't want to be blinded by all that dazzle and bling. And you'll want to conceal your sparkling eyes. If you get lucky you might glimpse the 128.54 carat Tiffany Yellow Diamond (aka Marilyn's BFF). And for a mere $12 million, you could even take it home.

㉑ TRUMP TOWER

725 5th Ave., between 56th and 57th St.
www.trumptowerny.com
🕐 Mo.-Su. 8 a.m.-10 p.m.

Don't be fooled. Donald (or is it Scrooge?) Trump is actually very modest. Gold just happens to be his favorite color and building towers is just another hobby. This is where he devised his plans to become president. The security and traffic jams after his unexpected election cost the city one million dollars a day. The bill was promptly sent to the White House.

㉒ POLO RALPH LAUREN

711 5th Avenue, Manhattan
visit5thavenue.com/ralphlauren
🕐 Mo.-Su. 10 a.m.-9 p.m.

Gray Ralph is usually at his ranch in Colorado but when he comes to New York, this is where you'll find him. In a hidden bar on the first floor you can have a cup of coffee with the most stylish man in the country.

㉓ MOMA

11 W 53rd St., between 5th and 6th Ave.
www.moma.org
🕐 Sa.-Th. 10:30 a.m. -5:30 p.m.,
Fr. 10:30 a.m.-8 p.m., closed
Thanksgiving Day and Christmas;
adults $25, seniors $18, students $14,
16 and under: free.

The MoMa is a fantastic museum; because of the art, of course, but also because of its excellent food. All thanks to Mrs. Rockefeller. Despite her family's swimming in money, she still had to search for sponsors to finance the MoMa. You see, Mr. Rockefeller was no big fan of modern art...

㉔ UNIQLO

666 5th Ave. and 53rd St.
www.uniqlo.com
🕐 Mo.-Sa. 10 a.m.-9 p.m.,
Su. 11 a.m.-8 p.m.

One of the largest stores on Fifth Avenue and the biggest UNIQLO worldwide. In case it hasn't sunk in: this store is huuuuuge. Thanks to its one hundred fitting rooms and fifty cash registers, you can be in and out in a flash. If you ever find the exit, that is.

㉕ ST. PATRICK'S CATHEDRAL

5th Ave., between 50th and 51st St.
www.saintpatrickscathedral.org
🕐 Daily 6:30 a.m.-8:45 p.m.

The largest Catholic church in the United States receives no fewer than five million visitors every year. One million of them light a candle. At least fifteen masses are held daily.

㉖ TOP OF THE ROCK

Rockefeller Center, 45 Rockefeller
Plaza, between 49th and 50th St. and
5th and 6th Ave.
www.topoftherocknyc.com
🕐 Daily 8 a.m.-midnight (last elevator
up at 11:15 p.m.); adults $34, seniors
(62+) $32, children (6 -12) $28.

What used to be the Rockefellers' private terrace offers an unequalled view of New York. The express elevators take you to the 67th floor in less than a minute. Make sure to look upwards on your way up.

㉗ AMERICAN GIRL

5th Ave. and 49th St.
www.americangirl.com
🕐 Mo.-Th. 10 a.m.-7 p.m.,
Fr. 10 a.m.-9 p.m., Sa. 9 a.m.-9 p.m.,
zo. 9 a.m.-7 p.m.

The concept is simple. You're broke and your kid is happy. Julie, Ruthie, Ivy, and Addy are just a few of the gorgeous dolls in this collection. The next American Girl will

undoubtedly be called Pretty Penny.

㉘ INTERNATIONAL GEM TOWER

50 West 47th St., between 5th and
6th Ave.

This gem in the diamond district was the work of my good friend Kim Van Holsbeke. As senior designer at architecture and design firm SOM, he belongs to the select circle of those who have planted a skyscraper in New York City. Respect!

㉙ BARNES & NOBLE

555 5th Ave., between 45th and
46th St.
store-locator.barnesandnoble.com/
store/2234
🕐 Mo.-Fr. 9 a.m.-9 p.m.,
Sa.-Su. 10 a.m.-9 p.m.

That's it! You've reached the end of the tour. If you need a good guide, this is the place. But you may just find that you're already holding the best one.

㉚ NBA STORE

545 5th Ave., between 44th and
45th St.
www.nba.com/nycstore
🕐 Mo.-Sa. 10 a.m.-9 p.m.,
Su. 11 a.m.-7 p.m.

The NBA Store is hallowed ground to basketball lovers. Actually, I first came across the store at 666 Fifth Avenue.

Exactly: UNIQLO's current address. They were prepared to shell out five times the rent the NBA Store was paying ($20 million a year).

MONICA

THE AMERICAN DREAM

"Oh, you are an actor? Which restaurant do you work at?"

The pull of the New York entertainment industry results in an overflow of talented (and not so talented) actors, singers, and dancers in the city. For many, a shot at immortality usually means just getting by on a badly paid restaurant or hotel job, all the while schlepping from audition to audition, hoping for the big break, which, with the exception of a select few, will never come.

In the days when I was the general manager of a restaurant this was an extra headache. The constant turnover of personnel, limited availability, lack of motivation and, often enough, lack of skill. Under these circumstances, Monica was a godsend.

Monica is Hungarian. Like many others, she crossed the Atlantic in search of her American dream. But, unlike most of her peers, Monica's future plans are to stick to the hospitality industry. Becoming famous is not on her agenda. Making money is. Which puts her in the exclusive and much-envied position of the professional waiter. She knows all the tricks of the trade and provides excellent service. She taught me countless knacks for getting better tips. These are essential skills in New York because the wages here are the pits, or close to it. What you bring home every evening is heavily dependent on the tips the customers leave you. Depending on the service, this would usually be between 15 and 20 percent. The more your customers consume, the more you stand to earn. The extra couple of dollars you make by offering bottled water instead of tap, doodling a smiley on the bill, laying a friendly hand on a customer, or making a well-placed joke can make a considerable difference at the end of the year. That goes without saying to someone like Monica. She repeatedly generated the most sales and was a great favorite with the customers. While her workmates were more focused on their next audition, Monica was practically running the whole restaurant singlehandedly.

Monica's ambition is to become a cocktail waitress at one of New York's most chic bars. Because that's where the big money is. At the moment, in order to get an early foot in the door, she's working in their cloakroom. Hopefully, her efforts will be rewarded and she'll land the well-paid job she's been American-dreaming of for so long.

A FEW TIPS FROM MONICA

GRATUITIES

Always check the restaurant bill closely. Many joints, especially in the heavily touristy areas, simply add the tip to the bill, despite its being officially forbidden. In such cases, the so-called 'gratuity' is already included and shouldn't be paid again separately. Otherwise, you'd be giving more than a double tip, which is not what you want, unless the service was that exceptional.

BROADWAY SHOW – THE LION KING

The Lion King is a must-see Broadway show in the Theater District's extensive repertoire. Experiencing a Broadway show is definitely a bucket list item and this one guarantees you a magical evening, replete with beautiful scenery, costumes, singing, and dancing.

A TIP FROM PATRICK

MUSICAL MARVELS

Broadway shows are New York's greatest cultural attraction and are of the highest quality. Talent from all over the world flocks to the Big Apple in hopes of securing a role in one of the many performances. Make no mistake; it's definitely worth the effort to let yourself be immersed in the magic of Broadway. Unfortunately, a ticket can sometimes cost an arm and a leg. When you know which show you'd like to see, try to get the tickets directly from the box office. My experience has taught me that the best prices are available there.

THE

RESTAURANT ABC

The range of places to eat in New York is immense. To help you choose your next meal, the New York State Department of Health issues an A (blue), B (green) or C (orange) to each establishment. With an A, you know you're safe and that you can expect everything to be neat and clean. B means there are several issues but none to be anxious about. When you encounter a C, it's best to keep in mind that there are at least as many rats living in the city as people. You sure don't want to meet one in your restaurant or, God forbid, on your plate. It is mandatory to display these labels, by the way, but you'll find spotting a B or a C often takes more scrutiny than most A's. Some restaurants find creative solutions for this requirement. One owner turned the regulation to his own advantage by promoting his brunch, adding 'runch' in the same font to his label.

HIGH QUALITY EATING OUT WITH A PINCH OF SALT

The rating system is a good indicator but a few footnotes are needed:

1. The classification refers only to food safety and says nothing about the culinary quality.
2. Many demerits that leave a restaurant with a low rating also have nothing to do with the food itself. A short distance between the kitchen and the restroom facilities or the absence of a lid on the garbage can could easily cost many points.
3. In addition, the system is "culturally discriminatory": Certain cuisines demand preparation methods that do not adhere to the Department of Health's requirements. For instance, Chinese kitchens were repeatedly slapped on the wrist for the temperature they used for preparing duck. That is, until a study showed it was a perfectly safe procedure. The same thing happened with the numerous sushi restaurants, where the chef traditionally and, as stated by the laws of the art, prepares the fish with his bare hands.

84% of all businesses eventually get the blue A, on condition that they pay the prerequisite and, often, considerable fines. Scandal-mongers call it more of a money-making machine for the city than a guarantee of quality for the customer.

RICHARD

HELP FROM THE GODFATHER

When I arrived to New York it was no bed of roses. Besides the daily hassles, I had one pretty major problem: my residence permit; better known as the *green card.*

I had only been married a year to the love of my life (at least, that's what I thought at the time) and that meant having to be subjected to questioning to find out if my marriage was for real. Unfortunately, we had never opened a joint bank account. On top of that, the lease was still in her name, I still had my Belgian health insurance and I had a suspicious lack of photos of the two of us. Barring a couple of love letters, I had no hard evidence of the authenticity of our relationship. And then came Richard. Through his connections, he found me a good lawyer who, just in time, sailed me through all the bureaucratic obstacles.

It was this same Richard who taught me how to network. No one knows better than he how difficult it is to achieve anything without knowing the right people. More than elsewhere, in New York "it's not what you know, it's who you know".

We called him the Godfather. Not inappropriately, considering his Italian roots. Richard isn't doing so bad and enjoys being everyone's guardian angel. He's a generous tipper and even had his own table at Petite Abeille, the restaurant I used to manage. This despite the *no reservation policy*. No matter how busy it was, Richard always got *his* table. And also his drink: Stoli with club soda, no ice, stirred. This was always waiting for him, even before he made his entrance. From busboy to manager, everyone knew Richard and enjoyed serving him. On particularly busy days, they would even text him to make sure that his spot needed to be kept free. Now that he's retired, there's a greater chance you'll see him having a good time at Petite Abeille. As he taught me: "Money talks, bullshit walks".

A TIP FROM RICHARD

THE PLAZA HOTEL

For a tasty breakfast, a nice brunch, or afternoon tea with cake you could go to the Plaza Hotel on the corner of 59th Street and 5th Avenue, just across from Central Park and the Apple Store. The beautiful interior, where scenes from Home Alone were filmed, will take your mind off the relatively steep prices.
www.theplazany.com/

A TIP FROM PATRICK

Underneath the Plaza Hotel there's a bona fide Food Hall. A stylishly designed, sprawling expanse housing a collection of refined culinary chefs(-d'oeuvre). Luke's Lobster is one of them. Its simple-sounding specialty is lobster in a bun, otherwise known as the Lobster Roll. But as simple as it sounds, the result is downright delicious and affordable too. Not surprisingly, Luke's Lobster was, upon opening in 2007, an overnight success.
www.theplazany.com/dining/foodhall/

AMERICA'S RUDEST CITY?

The bigger the city, the more arrogant its residents. If you believe this is true, then New Yorkers must be an extremely bad-mannered people. This is why readers of business magazine *Forbes* voted New York "most miserable city in the US." New York travel magazine *Travel+Leisure's* yearly poll of "America's Rudest Cities" has more than once reached the same conclusion. In 2015, New York topped the chart, followed by Miami, Washington, and Los Angeles. But *Travel+Leisure* had forgotten to ask how many of its voters had actually based their choice on their own experiences. Because, take it from me: the unfriendliness is a myth. It's true, New Yorkers are almost always

in a hurry and they don't have much time to hang around and smile at passing strangers. I wouldn't advise anyone to stand still on the sidewalk. But don't look twice if, in the subway, you see a heavy metal fan with a leather motorcycle jacket helping an Upper East Side mom carry her buggy up the stairs. This is normal. Also don't be surprised if, out of the blue, an East Villager asks your opinion about domestic politics or inquires about where you've already travelled and what you've seen. New Yorkers are extremely cordial and always curious.

NICE NEW YORKER

A young New Yorker named Ryan Beickert is on a mission to convince the world that New Yorkers aren't a bunch of unfriendly grouches. Every day he posts pictures of small gestures of friendliness on his website. Hearts etched into snow-covered cars, the sharing of umbrellas during sudden showers, or of water on sultry days. Witnessed a friendly gesture and had your phone or camera on hand? Don't wait to post it on Instagram or #nicenewyorker.
www.nicenewyorker.com

IF YOU CAN MAKE IT THERE...

...you'll make it anywhere. New Yorkers may be incredibly friendly but that still doesn't make New York an easy city to survive in. Not only does it have the greatest number of homeless people in the US, the most expensive colleges, the highest taxes, and insanely high rents, but you also freeze your butt off or sweat buckets for hours on the subway next to 5.4 million other people. But no pain, no gain. No other city in the world has spawned more stars and, to this day, Lady Liberty is still a magnet for anybody wanting to make it. Here is an A to Z of young talent that came here and tasted stardom not long afterwards.

A TIP FROM PATRICK

Go stand on the street with a city map and a camera and count the seconds before someone comes to your assistance. America's rudest city? No way!

CELEBRITY	OORSPRONG
Jennifer Aniston	Sherman Oaks, California
David Bowie	Brixton, Great Britain
Marlon Brando	Omaha, Nebraska
Michael Bloomberg	Boston, Massachusetts
Madonna Ciccone	Bay City, Michigan
Marlene Dietrich	Berlin, Germany
Bob Dylan	Duluth, Minnesota
Ella Fitzgerald	Newport News, Virginia
Greta Garbo	Stockholm, Sweden
Beyoncé Knowles	Houston, Texas
Spike Lee	Atlanta, Georgia
Ricky Martin	San Juan, Puerto Rico
Bette Midler	Honolulu, Hawaii
Nicky Minaj	Saint James, Trinidad and Tobago
Yoko Ono	Tokyo, Japan
Sarah Jessica Parker	Nelsonville, Ohio
Trixie Whitley	Ghent, Belgium

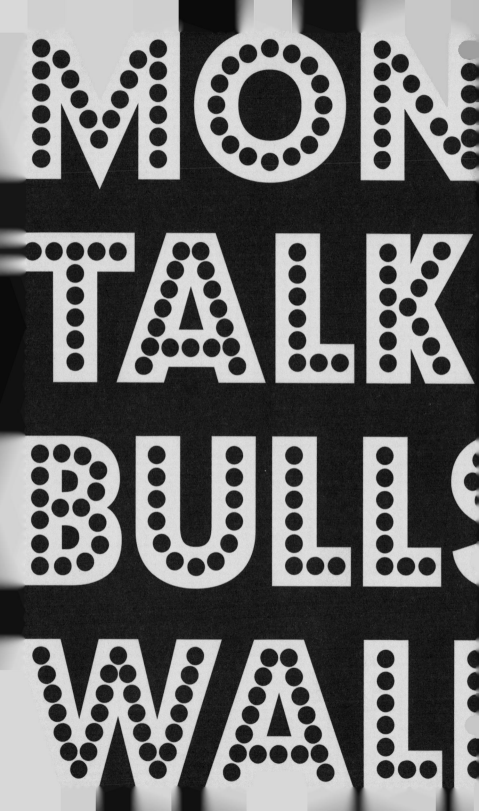

RICHARD

SEVEN & NATURALE

HIPSTER KIDS

These two rascals are the darlings of my good friend Arul (whose story appears later in this book). They are really sweet kids whose creativity has been stimulated as much as possible by their mother. Or by me, when mom is too busy with her business. We make paper planes or large drawings while my own darling baby, Marie, laughingly imitates us. So Seven and Naturale are getting a Belgian-American upbringing. They've learned to eat French fries the right way – with mayonnaise. And they pluck mussels from their shells with the previous one. The empty shells are then stacked neatly inside each other. When eating out, they know exactly what they want and they announce it explicitly. It always strikes me how polite and eloquent they are. Without a doubt, genuine little New Yorkers.

From birth, kids here learn to associate with other cultures, faiths, and languages. Chinese, African, Mexican... each class is a microcosm. And still, they manage to communicate. Because many nannies come from Latin America, there are many kids who are brought up with a basic knowledge of Spanish. There is respect not only for diversity but also for talent. It's really cute to see Seven and Naturale go wild to the tunes of a homeless musician in the subway. Being yourself and doing your own thing is encouraged here. It doesn't matter where you come from or how you look. Creativity must have free rein. Halloween is an ideal opportunity for stimulating it: pumpkin carving and trick-or-treating. And New York has the added advantage that one apartment building is enough for a year's supply of candy.

As a babysitter, you quickly learn all the kids' things to do in New York. For instance, I discovered the puppet theater in Central Park's Swedish Cottage. A totally "New York style" theater, including graffiti and rapping. I've also been through my fair share of playgrounds. In places like these you quickly become aware of the New Yorkers' watchfulness. And without a child, there's no way an adult can enter a playground. I also had to adjust to the differences compared to the easygoing European manners. For example, that a pat on a child's head, an innocent gesture to a Belgian, is out of the question here.

A TIP FROM SEVEN

SWEDISH COTTAGE MARIONETTE THEATRE
W 79th Street, Manhattan
The best puppet theater in town. The puppets here rap throughout the story and there's a view of Belvedere Castle, as seen in the movie "The Smurfs." Rumor has it that one day this gift from Sweden was converted into a public restroom. When Sweden got wind of this, they were so peeved that New York promptly turned it back into a puppet theater.

A TIP FROM NATURALE

AMERICAN GIRL
5th Ave. and 49th St.
www.americangirl.com
Choose a doll, dress her up, do her hair, and put on her makeup, ta-daa! There's something for every doll-lover in this paradise. They also have an incredible range of accessories. Your wish list sure won't get any shorter.

LA CUCARA-CHOCOLATE

I regularly delight my nephew Mathias with a present from magical New York. Such as an M&M's candy dispenser from their flagship store in Times Square. But upon opening the package, I discovered I had gotten more than I'd bargained for. A stowaway in the form of a giant cockroach had crossed the Atlantic with us. Later, when I filed a complaint with the store, I was allowed to choose an article from their range by way of compensation. Being a practiced New Yorker, I quickly turned things around: Let them choose a fitting form of compensation for the horrendous trauma inflicted on my nephew. And it worked. Not much later I received two giant boxes full of M&M's merchandise. Sometimes it's fun living in the land of litigation.

NEW YORK FOR KIDS

CHELSEA PIERS
23rd St. & Hudson River Park
www.chelseapiers.com
Bowling, golf, fitness, running, soccer, hockey, wall climbing, boxing, gymnastics, and much more. Sport and entertainment complex Chelsea Piers provides facilities for dozens of sports, including professional coaching if desired. Perfect for getting the kids out or for blowing off some steam.

SWEDISH COTTAGE
MARIONETTE THEATER
On Central Park's west side at 79th St.
www.cityparksfoundation. org/arts/swedish-cottage-marionette-theatre
The Swedish Cottage in Central Park has housed a

children's puppet theater since 1947. From classics such as Peter Pan to modern New York stories complete with raps and graffiti.

KIDDING AROUND

Grand Central Terminal, Lexington Passage, Manhattan
www.kiddingaroundtoys.com
Feel the need to get out sans kids but don't have the cash for an expensive babysitter? Amid the hustle and bustle of Grand Central Station is the smallest toy store in all of New York. Arts and crafts kits, music boxes, and unsolvable puzzles galore!

M&M'S STORE

1600 Broadway
www.mmsworld.com
At the M&M's flagship store north of Times Square you can find M&M's in every conceivable color. On the

first floor, you can even have them personalized with your own text or drawing. Or use a picture of yourself to prove how irresistible you are.

DYLAN'S CANDY BAR

1011, 3rd Ave.
www.dylanscandybar.com
Ralph Lauren's daughter apparently inherited her father's sense of entrepreneurship (his bank

account probably helps too). Inspired by Willy Wonka, she opened a candy store on the Upper East Side, which unifies candy pop culture and fashion. This three-story Shangri-La for the sweet tooth has a range of 7,000 types of confectionery. And in the basement, Dylan's Barbie double adorns the extensive Candy Bar

Celebrity Wall. This wall reveals the tastes of a whole slew of celebrities who have been tempted by this store's delights. Your teeth have been duly warned.

ALICE IN WONDERLAND

E 74th St., Central Park
This bronze work of art was inspired by the figures from *Alice in Wonderland*. It was a gift to the children of New York and is meant to be climbed.

CENTRAL PARK ZOO

64th St.and 5th Ave.
A jaunt to this small-scale zoo in the middle of Central Park is a bull's eye for the little ones. It has more than 130 different species of animal, including snow leopards, penguins, and sea lions. You can even have your birthday party catered there. The cheapest party on their list starts at $5,000. Maybe just settle for a ticket.

SEAN LYNCH

COMEDIAN, STAND UP

Anyone who wanders around Times Square can't escape being asked whether they like comedy. It's a clever bait to talk you into buying tickets, because who doesn't like a good laugh? Still, there's a big difference between what they try to palm off on you and the *real* New York *comedy scene*. Just ask my good friend Sean, who's been a comedian for years.

Sean had already made it when he was young. He promptly got a job as a voice actor and was also one of the driving forces behind MTV's Celebrity Death Match. Unfortunately, his career experienced a setback when he lost two of his comedy group friends to the 9/11 attacks. His sense of humor was buried with them under the rubble and he put his stand-up comedy career on hold for a long time.

But old habits die hard and Sean fought his way back onstage. Successfully. He masters the art of turning hard reality into lighthearted entertainment. He now uses this art to crack people up all over the country. Like the time Sean was robbed. *Not a big deal* in New York, according to Sean. He had dozed off in the subway on the way to Harlem and when he awoke, he was particularly impressed by the skillful way a 16-year-old was cutting his wallet out of his pants. Rather than protest, Sean asked his assailant whether he'd ever been to the DMV (Department of Motor Vehicles). He could keep the money. But would he do Sean a favor and let him keep his driver's license and spare him a return visit to that administrative hell? The mugger agreed and handed over the driver's license before disappearing with the rest of Sean's possessions.

I myself was also a source of inspiration. I discovered this when Sean invited me to one of his shows. He had somehow forgotten to mention that just about his whole *routine* that evening was about me. *Patrick the Belgian* even found his way on to the silver screens of the International Film Festival Manhattan as one of the characters in Sean's short film.

A TIP FROM SEAN

Don't fall for the comedy shows they try to palm off on you in Times Square. The quality is not up to par and the standard is inversely proportional to the price. If you want to experience respectable stand-up, go to the Broadway Comedy Club. The owner used to be a comedian himself and hand-picks all the performers. The prices are reasonable too.

www.broadwaycomedyclub.com

FUN FACT

Most of the comedy show tickets vendors in Times Square are, in fact, comedians. For a certain number of tickets sold, they're granted a minute on stage. The club owners care more about sold-out rooms than about quality. But the big question is: Are the best peddlers also the funniest?

COMEDY

New York has a comedy tradition stretching back decades and the city is, to this day, the Mecca for America's comedians. Besides an abundance of comedy clubs, there are live recordings of popular TV shows, such as *Saturday Night Live*, *The Daily Show* and *The Tonight Show*. If you're lucky you could still catch Jerry Seinfeld, the most popular TV comedian in American history, at work here and there. Since the last episode of his very New York-ish sitcom *Seinfeld*, broadcast in 1998 and viewed by 80 million Americans, the comedian has been taking it relatively easy. But occasionally he could still hop onstage unannounced anywhere, such as the Gotham Comedy Club.

THE NAKED COWBOY

After more than ten years, he has become part of the scenery in Times Square. The Naked Cowboy (don't worry, he still wears his underpants) became popular in no time and has also inspired many imitators. Now, Times Square features a Naked Indian and even a Naked Granny. The Naked Cowboy is also married to one of the Naked Cowgirls who occasionally accompany him.

Political aspirations ensued. Robert Burck (his real name) announced he'd run for mayor and later even became a candidate for the presidential elections. That was reaching a bit too far but he's still doing great business. He still shows up daily in Times Square and recently even released an album. If you would like to be joined in marriage by the "Reverend" Naked Cowboy, ceremonies are possible from $499. He can be reached at +1-866-99-NAKED.

COUNTERFEIT CLERICS

Times Square is loaded with pseudo Buddhist monks. They hand out amulets or talismans in exchange for a donation. Usually for the construction of a new temple in some obscure, faraway country. A client of mine was once approached this way. He trustingly gave the "monk" $5. The latter inquired about his country of origin, thumbed his little book and promptly declared that the rate for Belgians was $20. Fortune favors the bold.

A TIP FROM PATRICK

Situated at the very top of the famous Marriott Marquis hotel on Times Square is The View restaurant and lounge. The magnificent panorama afforded here changes continuously, thanks to the 360-degree revolving floor. The view is way up there, as are the prices.
www.theviewnyc.com

COMEDY CLUBS

COMIC STRIP
1568 2nd Ave.
www.comicstriplive.com
Comic Strip is the oldest comedy club in the world. Eddie Murphy's career was launched here, as were Jerry Seinfeld's and Adam Sandler's. And what about Ellen DeGeneres, Jimmy Fallon, Chris Rock, Jon Stewart, Sarah Silverman, and Wanda Sykes? They all graced this stage. Comic Strip remains one of the most important venues where young talent is discovered. Very schedule-friendly too, being open nightly.

THE CREEK AND THE CAVE
10-93 Jackson Ave.,
Long Island City, Queens
www.creeklic.com
This famous comedy club is located in Queens, one stop away from Grand Central (on line 7). This club is also open every evening for your entertainment (usually between 6 and 10 p.m.). You also stand a chance of catching Seinfeld, who is regularly spotted here.

NEVADA

UTAH

CALIFORNIA

ARIZONA

DID YOU KNOW THAT THE
POPULATION
DENSITY OF NEW YORK
IS SO HIGH THAT IF
TEXAS WERE SO DENSELY POPULATED,
THE ENTIRE POPULATION
OF THE WORLD
COULD FIT INSIDE ITS BORDERS?

SOUTH DAKOTA
MINNESOTA
WYOMING
IOWA
NEBRASKA
COLORADO
KANSAS
MISSOURI
OKLAHOMA
NEW MEXICO
ARKANSAS
LOUISIANA
GULF OF MEXICO

EVOLVING NEW YORK
THE VILLAGES

EVOLVING NEW YORK
THE VILLAGES

🕐 4 TO 5 HOURS

1. EMPIRE STATE BUILDING
2. MACY'S
3. MADISON SQUARE GARDEN
4. JAMES FARLEY POST OFFICE BUILDING
5. HUDSON YARDS
6. HIGH LINE
7. IAC
8. HAUSER & WIRTH
9. MORIMOTO
10. THE LOBSTER PLACE
11. GIOVANNI RANA PASTIFICIO & CUCINA
12. DIANE VON FURSTENBERG
13. THE STANDARD GRILL
14. CHRISTIAN LOUBOUTIN
15. FELLOW BARBER
16. CORNER BISTRO
17. MAGNOLIA BAKERY
18. BOBO
19. THE STONEWALL INN
20. THE GARRET
21. JOE'S PIZZA
22. MONTE'S TRATTORIA
23. MAMOUN'S FALAFEL
24. OTTO ENOTECA E PIZZERIA
25. WASHINGTON SQUARE PARK
26. TISCH SCHOOL OF ARTS
27. GRACE CHURCH
28. MCSORLEY'S OLD ALE HOUSE
29. PDT (PLEASE DON'T TELL)
30. DEATH & COMPANY

New York is changing quickly. Even those who live here have a hard time keeping up-to-date. If you return to a neighborhood after a couple of weeks, you'll find new buildings have sprung up, restaurants have disappeared, parks have been laid, and streets have been refurbished. You can move quickly from one neighborhood to the next in New York. Walk a couple of blocks and you're in a totally different environment. This walk takes you through neighborhoods in various stages of development. You will cross the budding Hudson Yards, the maturing Chelsea, and the much riper Villages. Each has its own look and feel, inhabitants and history. The only constant is change. If you stop to think about, it you'll see: New York is on the move.

❶ EMPIRE STATE BUILDING

5th Ave. and 34th St.

www.esbnyc.com

🕐 Mo.-Su. 8 a.m.-2 a.m.

This monument dominates Midtown Manhattan and helps with orientation. It's impossible to miss. This building is so big it has its own ZIP Code. The Empire State Building was completed in 1931 on the spot of the Waldorf & Astoria hotels. Since zeppelins were still "hot" in those days, the top of this skyscraper was designed as a docking station for dirigibles. Meanwhile, the tower gets struck by lightning an average of 23 times a year.

❷ MACY'S

151 W 34th St., between 5th and 6th Ave.

www.macys.com

🕐 Mo.-Fr. 9 a.m.-9:30 p.m., Sa. 10 a.m.-9:30 p.m., Su. 11 a.m.-8:30 p.m.

This mammoth needs no introduction. With its seven million cubic feet holding more than four million items, America's largest department store attracts more than 20 million shopaholics annually. Happen to have a foreign passport? That gives you a 10% discount.

❸ MADISON SQUARE GARDEN

Between 31st and 33rd St. and 7th and 8th Ave.

www.thegarden.com

Madison Square Garden is on 8th Avenue (not Madison), is round (not square), and is a concert hall (not a garden). It changed locations several times before finally settling where Penn Station once stood in all its glory. The demolition of this phenomenal station to make way for The Garden led to the establishment of the Landmarks Preservation Commission in the hope of preventing similar blunders in the future.

❹ JAMES FARLEY POST OFFICE BUILDING

412 8th Ave. between 31st St. and 33rd St.

www.usps.com

🕐 Mo.-Fr. 7 a.m.-10 p.m., Sa. 9 a.m.-9 p.m., Su. 11 a.m.-7 p.m.

This massive building, across from The Garden, has been mostly vacant since the advent of e-mail and other modern means of communication. There are plans to house newer incarnations of both Penn Station and Madison Square Garden here. The vacated site will serve as ground for brand new skyscrapers, since there's such a shortage of them in New York...

❺ HUDSON YARDS

www.hudsonyardsnewyork.com

Between 30th and 33rd St. and 10th and 12th Ave.

The west side of Manhattan is at its peak of development. There are enormous plans for this part of the city. Hudson Yards is the largest construction project since the Rockefeller Center and the largest private project development in US history. A magnificent work of art, which bears a striking resemblance to a gigantic kebab, will be placed at its center. Construction is due to be completed by 2019.

6 HIGH LINE

Between Gansevoort St. and W 34th St.
www.thehighline.org
⏱ Dec.-Mar. 7 a.m-7 p.m., Apr., May, Oct., and Nov. 7 a.m.-10 p.m., June-Sep. 7 a.m.-11 p.m.

The railroad tracks originally ran through 10th Avenue, which was then also called Death Avenue due to the large number of accidents. This was solved by raising the line and by putting up warehouses. By the end of the 1980s, the railway had fallen into disuse and it was decided to turn it into a park. A successful initiative, receiving much praise from tourists, from the local residents enjoying the upgrade, and from local real estate owners.

7 IAC

555 W 18th St.
www.iac.com

This building is a 2007 creation as well as the New York debut of the well-known architect, Frank Gehry, of the Bilbao Guggenheim fame. It was one of the first new High Line projects, a forerunner of many more. It serves as the headquarters of internet corporation InterActive-Corp, owner of an array of popular websites such as Vimeo, About.com, Ask. com, Collegehumor, Match.com, Tinder, OkCupid, etc.

8 HAUSER & WIRTH

511 W 18th St. between 10th and 11th Ave.
www.hauserwirth.com
⏱ Tu.-Sa. 10 a.m.-6 p.m.

This gallery resides in what used to be roller-skating disco The Roxy: A nightlife monument graced by the likes of Madonna, Cher, and Whitney Houston. Nowadays it's strictly an art venue but the rink's recessed surface bears silent witness to a stormy past.

9 MORIMOTO

88 W 10th Ave.
www.morimotonyc.com
⏱ Mo.-We. noon-2:30 p.m. and 5:30p.m.-11 p.m., Th.-Fr. until midnight, Sa. 5:30p.m.- midnight, Su. 5:30p.m.-10 p.m.

Iron Chef Masaharu Morimoto wields the authority (and the sushi knives) in a formal, modern setting, which draws the Casual Chic crowd. You really need to go to the bathroom here. Not because of the food, but because this fully automatic commode was once voted Best Toilet of the Year.

10 THE LOBSTER PLACE

75 9th Ave., in Chelsea Market
www.lobsterplace.com
⏱ Mo.-Sa. 9:30 a.m.-9 p.m., Su. 10 a.m.-8 p.m.

If you can't make up your mind from the selection of fish, shellfish, and crustaceans available here, you won't be able to anywhere. The Lobster Place is so immaculate and of such high quality that I wouldn't dare call it a fish market. Before you know it, you're headed home with a freshly steamed lobster or a delicious lobster roll. There's more to life than hamburgers.

11 GIOVANNI RANA PASTIFICIO & CUCINA

75 9th Ave., in Chelsea Market
www.rananyc.com
⏱ Mo.-Sa. 11 a.m.-11 p.m., Su. 11 a.m.-10 p.m.

Rana is one of my favorite restaurants: Respectable, affordable, and authentic Italian. Giovanni Rana was actually an engineer and he succeeded in creating a machine that could perfectly simulate the manual kneading of pasta dough. His invention is on display in the Pasta Studio, As is the red moped on which Giovanni delivered his homemade pasta in his hometown of Verona, fifty years ago. It gained him popularity envied even by the Pope *and* a restaurant in hip Chelsea.

⑫ DIANE VON FURSTENBERG

874 Washington St., corner of 14th St.

www.dvf.com

🕐 Mo.-We. and Fr.-Sa. 11a.m.-7 p.m.,
Th. 11 a.m.-8 p.m., Su. noon-6 p.m.

She adorns a myriad of taxis, billboards, guest lists, and honor rolls. Since her divorce, she is no longer a princess, but Ms. von Furstenberg is still the queen of fashion. Notables such as Jennifer Lopez, Madonna, and Michelle Obama have been spotted wearing her creations. The headquarters and flagship store of this fashion diva from Brussels are located near the High Line. The von Furstenberg Family Foundation must be happy with the park since it has donated $35 million to its development.

⑬ THE STANDARD GRILL

848 Washington St.

www.thestandardgrill.com

🕐 Mo.-Th. noon-3 p.m. and 7 p.m.-midnight, Fr.-Su. noon-4 p.m. and 7 p.m.-midnight

A congenial restaurant with dishes on the menu that quickly help you forget the numbers next to them. The wine list is just as ambitious and pricey. Reserve early if you want to sit in the dining room. The empty tables in the front are there for a reason: It's so noisy there that conversation is virtually impossible.

⑭ CHRISTIAN LOUBOUTIN

59 Horatio St.

www.christianlouboutin.com

🕐 Mo.-Sa. 11 a.m.-7 p.m.,
Su. noon-6 p.m.

Slow down, ladies! I hope you have saved up enough for new shoes – with or without the typical red soles – and matching handbag.

⑮ FELLOW BARBER

5 Horatio St.

www.fellowbarber.com

🕐 Mon.-Fri. 9 a.m.-9 p.m.,
Sa.-Su. 9 a.m.-6 p.m.

Fellow Barber has filled the gap in the market for affordable hair care combined with the service of a hair salon. Mike – who looks a little like Robert de Niro – and his colleagues can give you a snazzy New York haircut. So, now that you look cool, you're ready to hit the streets with enough cash left for a matching outfit.

⑯ CORNER BISTRO

331 W 4th St.

www.cornerbistrony.com

🕐 Mo.-Sa. 11 a.m.-4 p.m., Su. noon-4 p.m.

The interior ain't much to look at but the burgers are damn good. Period.

⑰ MAGNOLIA BAKERY

401 Bleecker St., between Perry St. and W 11th St.

www.magnoliabakery.com

🕐 Mo.-Th. 9 a.m.-11:30 p.m.,
Fr. and Sa. 9 a.m.-12:30 a.m.,
Su. 9 a.m.- 11:30 p.m.

Welcome to cupcake paradise, where everything is handmade. You can even have your own design put on a cake. But watch out! The selection and the quality have reduced many an envious grandma to tears. Moreover, drooling is unavoidable and if you wet it, you own it.

⑱ BOBO

181 W 10th St., corner of 7th Ave.

www.bobonyc.com

🕐 Mo.-Th. 6 p.m.-11 p.m., Fr. until midnight, Sa. 11 a.m.-3 p.m. and 6 p.m.-midnight, Su. until 10 p.m.

This beautifully fashioned little restaurant is a hidden gem with a small but very cozy patio in back, offering a relaxed atmosphere. The dishes aren't exotic but are prepared creatively and tastefully. A large helping of friendliness (to clients and wallet) completes the fine picture. Perfect for a romantic dinner.

⑲ THE STONEWALL INN

53 Christopher St., between 7th Ave. and Waverly

www.thestonewallinnnyc.com

🕐 Mo.-Su. 2 p.m.-4 a.m.

This is where the homonymous riots broke out in 1969 between the police and the LGBT community, fighting for equal rights. Just ask the manager, who still regularly tends the bar. All the current Gay Pride marches worldwide are a direct result of this demonstration. Monday evenings is drag queen bingo night. The witty remarks they hurl at you can be eased by the alcohol you win. I'm sure you'll have a gay old time!

⑳ THE GARRET

7th Ave. and Barrow St.

www.garretnyc.com

🕐 Mo.-We. 5 p.m.-1 a.m., Th. and Fr. 5 p.m.-2 a.m., Sa. noon-2 a.m., Su. noon-1 a.m.

The Garret is something between a sports bar and a speakeasy. It used to be a sports cafe with the customary TV screens on the walls. Now they assume a homey mood with cocktails. But the screen is still there and the place is packed during major games. Ideal for the distinguished sports lover who can guzzle half a dozen vodka martinis first, before damning the umpire's biased eyes. The Garret is located above the Five Guys burger joint. Not difficult to find but it helps to know.

㉑ JOE'S PIZZA

7 Carmine St. between Bleecker and 6th Ave.

www.joespizzanyc.com

🕐 Mo.-Sa. 10 a.m.-4:30 a.m., Su. until 4 a.m.

This pizzeria also claims the title of "Best Pizza in New York." Its assertion is supported by Kevin Spacey, who, judging from the pictures on the walls, drops by regularly. Admittedly, the pizza is fine but for $3.50 per slice, don't expect any miracles. Let's just call it a reasonable, quick bite and a case of an actor who probably got the munchies after living up to his family name.

㉒ MONTE'S TRATTORIA

97 Macdougal St., between Minetta and Bleecker

www.montestrattorianyc.com

🕐 Su.-Th. noon-11 p.m. (Tu. closed), Fr.-Sa. noon-11:30 a.m.

This is the Italian restaurant where Joey from Friends took his dates and once even a double date with Chandler. Though this was probably unintentional. No frivolous culinary spectacles on the menu, just classic Italian. Since 1918.

㉓ MAMOUN'S FALAFEL

119 Macdougal St., between W 3rd and Minetta

www.mamouns.com

🕐 Mo.-Su. 11 a.m.-5 a.m.

Cheap food joints abound in the student neighborhoods. Such as Mamoun's Falafel, where you can get a delicious falafel for $2.50. If you enjoy a challenge and spicy food: Mamoun is known for his ridiculously spicy hot sauce. Try it one drop at a time and proceed at your own risk.

㉔ OTTO ENOTECA E PIZZERIA

1 5th Ave.

www.ottopizzeria.com

🕐 Mo.-Su. 11:30 a.m.-midnight

Mario Batali is a well-known chef and TV personality with a line of Italian-inspired restaurants in Hong Kong, Singapore, and New York. The fairly large Otto in the West Village is one of these. With its reasonable prices and good quality, it is an attractive option for larger company.

㉕ WASHINGTON SQUARE PARK
5th Ave., Waverly Pl., W. 4 St., and Macdougal St.
www.nycgovparks.org

No park deserves the term "buzzing" more than Washington Square Park. It may once have been a cemetery but it's certainly no stiff joint. This is thanks to the many students studying art, literature, drama, dance, or music at NYU and who come here to live it up. They even drag pianos and drum sets to the park. Other interesting activities are feeding pigeons, cooling off in the fountain, and playing chess against homeless people. For just a couple of bucks they'll gladly take you to the cleaners.

㉖ TISCH SCHOOL OF ARTS
721 Broadway
tisch.nyu.edu

Ambitions to launch a Broadway career? Get started here in the footsteps of Woody Allen, Martin Scorsese, Alec Baldwin, James Franco, Whoopi Goldberg, and a whole lot more celebrities.

㉗ GRACE CHURCH
802 Broadway and E 10th St.
www.gracechurchnyc.org
🕐 Mo.-Su. noon-5 p.m.

This Neo-Gothic church has a history going back more than 200 years. It was designed by James Renwick Jr., who would grow into one of the most successful American architects of his time. He later also designed the renowned St. Patrick's Cathedral on 5th Avenue. Slip in for a quick confession so you can paint the town red with a clean conscience.

㉘ MCSORLEY'S OLD ALE HOUSE
15 E 7th St., between 2nd Ave. and Cooper Sq.
mcsorleysoldalehouse.nyc
🕐 Mo.-Sa. 11 a.m.-1 a.m., Su. 1 p.m.-1 a.m.

Historic! What else would you call a tavern where even Abraham Lincoln went for a brewski? Nothing has changed in more than a century. Even the wishbones hung on the lamps by WWI soldiers are still there. As are Houdini's handcuffs. Before the Supreme Court's involvement in 1970, women were not welcome at McSorley's and that included the proprietress! Choosing your beer is easy since there are only two options: light or dark. Cheers!

㉙ PDT (PLEASE DON'T TELL)
113 St. Marks Pl.
www.pdtnyc.com
🕐 Su.-Th. 6 p.m.-2 a.m., Fr.-Sa. 6 p.m.-3 a.m.

A good spot for both hotdogs and cocktails, depending on what time it is when you saunter in. If you want the latter, you'll need to use the phone booth. First, to gain entrance to the cocktail bar beyond it and, second, to call home and let them know you will be a little late.

㉚ DEATH & COMPANY
433 E 6th St. between Ave. A and 1st Ave.
www.deathandcompany.com
🕐 Su.-Th. 6 p.m.-1 a.m., Fr. and Sa. 6 p.m.-2 a.m.

Here too, things don't start to get going until the evening. This well-known speakeasy owes its popularity to the cool vibe and interior. Unfortunately, there is limited room. So get there early or be prepared to wait for a table.

Danny

HOT FOOD, COLD FEET

In addition to being a top chef and TV personality, Danny Boome is also a very easy-going, good-natured, and ambitious guy who made New York his home more than ten years ago. He lends his expertise to a variety of cooking shows in the US and Canada and has an incomparable knowledge of the culinary world.

His predilection for the Belgian kitchen often brought him to Petite Abeille, where we brainstormed for hours about possible food tours through the city. He constantly pushed me to try out new restaurants and would often come up with new and interesting places. Thanks to him, when I was just starting my business, I already knew which restaurants to book for my clients. An elaborate business lunch, a birthday party in a family restaurant, a romantic dinner with your betrothed... New York offers thousands of options for any occasion. And in the interest of the client, I naturally have to test them all beforehand...

He also deserves the credit for my initiation into Super Bowl rituals.

A few years ago Danny invited me to a party in SoHo to celebrate the Solemn Mass of American sport. In the luxury apartment of one of his good friends, everything followed the tradition: someone puts their home at everyone's disposal and they all show up with mountains of food and drink. Danny was, due in no small part to his culinary skills, always a desired guest. Of course the Belgian beers were on me.

We became such good friends that he even invited me to his wedding party. A party, which, in accordance with family drama rules, he cancelled just before the ceremony. I learned about it over the phone, when he called me, begging me to help him by receiving and showing around his family, who had especially flown over from the United Kingdom for the party. I was to provide them with alternative activities. Yet another of the varied tasks of your city tour guide...

Over the period that followed we very often went out together so he could keep his mind on other things and to help him process the dramatic events. In the neighborhood where I was living at the time – the Upper East Side – there were, according to the statistics, two women to every man (and, if we factor out the considerable gay community in New York, that would be more in the range of 3 to 1) so things were moving fast. Maybe a bit too fast. Three months later, he was informed that he had six months to prepare for fatherhood. In an unexpected turn of events, he was on his way to family life again. That family is still around today and he is the happiest father in all of New York. Except me, of course. How quickly life can change.

A Tip from Danny

BABBO RISTORANTE E ENOTECA
110 Waverly Place, between McDougal St. and 6th Ave.
www.babbonyc.com
Right next to Washington Square Park is the Michelin-starred Italian restaurant, Babbo. Here, you are treated to the best of Italian cuisine, made mostly with ingredients imported from Italy. The key word from the above is "Michelin", not "treated". I don't want to raise any false hopes before you're presented with the bill. Quality doesn't come cheap but your taste buds will have a party. Reservations are necessary.

BLUE RIBBON BAKERY
35 Downing St.
www.blueribbonrestaurants.com
If you're looking for a delicious brunch, drop by (read: make reservations) the Blue Ribbon. Blue Ribbon restaurants have a good reputation and this one in the West Village keeps up that reputation. The restaurants score highly with their delectable homemade bread, an item not always easy to find in New York. If you just can't get enough of it, you can buy more at the Blue Ribbon Bakery Market, just across the street. Yum!

A Tip from Patrick

ROCKWOOD

196 Allan St., between Houston and Stanton
www.rockwoodmusichall.com

Rockwood has most definitely become
one of my favorite music venues since
I first went there with Danny. At this
cool place on the Lower East Side you
can get your kicks every day on *hot* live
music played on three different stages.
I actually had the honor of hearing Selah
Sue (A Belgian musician and songwrit-
er) here. You have to pay for some shows
but the prices are always reasonable; for
the drinks too. This odeon has spawned
so much talent that, if you're a music
lover, you just can't pass it up.

Pizza in New York

Anyone who has ever been to Italy may well ask how New York dares call itself the pizza capital of the world. You better ask it silently because New Yorkers take their pizza tradition very seriously. And you gotta hand it to them, they really do have delicious pizza. Some more good advice: always eat pizza with your hands. When Bill de Blasio, in his first year as New York's mayor, actually had the audacity to eat a pizza with a knife and fork, he was the laughingstock of the press for days.

TWO BOOTS PIZZA
(various locations, including Grand Central)
www.twoboots.com
This is my favorite pizza place. It's a successful combination of Cajun (South Louisiana) and Italian. There are several branches in the city and each Two Boots has its own specialties. It's simply good-tasting pizza at a reasonable price and "by the slice" – the New York way.

ROBERTA'S PIZZA
261 Moore St., between White St. and Bogart St., East Williamsburg/Bushwick, Brooklyn
www.robertaspizza.com
For cool pizza, rush on over to Roberta's in Bushwick. You can immediately tell you're in Brooklyn just by glancing at the clientele. Delicious pizza and hip to boot. The Bee Sting – pizza with honey and chili peppers – is their most famous pie.

99 CENT PIZZA
All over the city.
No culinary epiphany, but definitely good for a quick, cheap bite. Especially in a city as expensive as New York. These pizza parlors do massive overtime, especially in the student neighborhoods, but, these days, you can find them just about everywhere. Not something for every day, but the perfect solution when you need to chow down in a hurry.

Street Meat

The streets of New York are swarming with food stands and, for many a New Yorker, a visit to them is part of the daily routine. Food trucks are safe and part of the *New York experience*. So be sure to drop by the Halal Guys, the Big Gay Ice Cream Truck or, my own national pride and joy, Wafels & Dinges (Belgian for "Waffles and Stuff"). Note: you don't eat waffles here *without* the stuff or with just some of it. So, if you don't mind, please pile on the strawberries, banana and walnut, *speculaas* butter, a scoop of vanilla ice cream with whipped cream, Belgian chocolate, some Nutella, syrup, and powdered sugar. Medical insurance is optional, seventh heaven is guaranteed. Be careful with the smallest street stands! Not much can go wrong with a pretzel or a hotdog, but chicken or other meat doesn't always get sufficiently cooked on those tiny grills, which increases the chance of salmonella rearing its ugly head. Also, if you buy a drink, always check if the top is sealed, especially with water bottles. Cans are always a safer option.

SMALL CARTS, BIG BUSINESS

The stands may be small but the sums involved are anything but. The most expensive *food cart* zones are in Central Park. To be able to sell hotdogs there, on the corner of Fifth Avenue and East 62nd Street, you have to shell out $289,500 a year. This must mean that each year at least 144,750 people walk by in dire need of a $2 hotdog. All the same, it's a lot of money – especially considering that ten years ago the same location "only" cost $120,000.

YELP vs Michelin

Michelin stars have lost none of their prestige over the years but modern times have definitely brought a change in restaurant reviews. Now, websites such as YELP, Zagat, and TripAdvisor are also awarding stars. Particularly due to the number of users, these sites give a more accurate picture of what you can expect from your restaurant or cafe of choice. Moreover, the information is more up-to-date and the list much longer. For New Yorkers, these sites are the standard reference for choosing where to consume their next meal. A handful of good or bad reviews can make or break a restaurant's reputation in no time. As a city guide, I advise everyone to take advantage of these useful resources and always to sniff out the most recently circulating praise or criticism of the place you intend to go to. Forewarned is forearmed!
www.yelp.com — www.zagat.com — www.tripadvisor.com

Chisum

HAUTE COFFEE CUISINE

Coffee culture in New York has mushroomed. You can get a caffeine hit literally on every street corner. Not for nothing does Starbucks have more branches here than McDonald's (where you can also get coffee, by the way). And then there are the other chains such as Dunkin' Donuts, 7/11, etc. Not to mention the range of small, trendy coffee joints, which, if you ask the New Yorkers, is where they really know how to make a good cup of coffee. But the stuff Chisum brews in her tiny place in the East Village will really knock your socks off.

I consider myself lucky to be married to a blog mom who closely follows what's going on in the city. Thanks to her, in my very limited free time, I can still drop by a place I didn't know. That's how I discovered The Coffee Project, a super cool nook of a shop where Chisum and her partner Kaleena run the show. Chisum is a new kid on the New York block, especially compared with me. In 2012 she left Klang, the largest port city in Malaysia, for this pleasant marina on the Hudson. It's been only five years but her business is up and running. But what do you expect with such a groundbreaking concept? Chisum serves a "deconstructed" latte. That means a latte divided into three glasses, to be drunk according to the prescribed ritual. First, you drink a small shot of espresso, then a shot of steamed milk and, to top it off, foamed milk. An amazing coffee experience! Or try the Nitro Coffee: bubbling, cold draft coffee; a celebration for your taste buds. All the while Chisum and Kaleena are there to answer any question. That's what's so great about New York: even the most commonplace things are transformed into original and unknown specialties!

A Tip from Chisum

ATTABOY
134 Eldridge St, between Broome & Delancey on the Lower East Side
This concealed bar, or speakeasy, houses topnotch mixologists (the correct New York title for cocktail artists). And topnotch drinks. If you want to have your mind professionally expanded in a non-touristy setting, then Attaboy is highly recommended.

Go nuts for cronuts

Two months and ten different recipes were needed to perfect the cronut. This delicious cross between a croissant and a donut is the – now patented – brainchild of New Yorker Dominique Ansel. The cronut became immensely popular in no time and has a massive worldwide following. Many imitations have now sprung up but for the one and only genuine cronut you have to go to the Dominique Ansel Bakery on Spring Street, SoHo.

Dominique Ansel Bakery
189 Spring Street, SoHo
www.dominiqueansel.com

In order to taste this delicacy you have to roll out of bed early. I can personally testify to this. The bakery can only produce a limited amount every day and sometimes people will wait in line for two hours to get their hands on the maximum of two cronuts per person. For me, this meant getting in line at 4:30 a.m. I had to satisfy my curiosity at all costs. In terms of price: besides infinite patience, this treasure usually costs $5. But the short supply has created a black market where a cronut could go for as high as $100. All that hype makes the second half of the name extra appropriate. And, yes, it was good. But to say it was worth the hassle... Just give me a nice Belgian waffle with lots of whipped cream!

Breakfast in New York

ESS-A-BAGEL

There is nothing more typical New York than a good bagel. This roll with a hole comes in a wide variety: with poppy or sesame seeds, multigrain, rye or whole wheat, toasted or not, and so on. Ess-a-bagel's products have harvested a *hole* lot of prizes and honorable mentions. How about a toasted, hand-rolled bagel with lox, cream cheese, tomato, and spring onions for a good start to the day?

ess-a-bagel.com

MAISON KAISER

The name alone gives away the French connection. Maison Kayser has, in fact, come over from Paris. If you spot their tasteful logo at one of the ten current locations all over the city, don't hesitate: go in and treat yourself to a divine breakfast of the most exquisite soft-boiled eggs, croissants, and baguettes. And don't deny it: you were immediately sold when you saw their assortment of luscious pastries. Get ready to count your calories!

www.maison-kayser-usa.com

Coffee places in New York

If coffee beans ceased to exist, life in New York would grind to a complete halt. New Yorkers drink up to six times as much coffee as residents of other metropolises and they pay three times as much for it as the average American, without blinking an eye. Moreover, in 2013, more than 300,000 New Yorkers participated in The World's Largest Coffee Break. Not so good for the American economy; not so bad for the Colombian.

ROASTING PLANT

81 Orchard St. (and other locations)
www.roastingplant.com
Here, the coffee beans literally whizz by, through the ingenious tube system of the JavaBot. This coffee machine takes up the whole store and grinds and brews your selected coffee blend within 30 seconds. It can't get any fresher than that!

HAPPY BONES

394 Broome St.
www.happybonesnyc.com
Coffee is an ideology here. Happy Bones collaborates, as much as possible, directly with the coffee farmers and recycles to the max. A share of the profits goes to charity.

Green, ethically responsible, fair-trade coffee and delicious to boot. Enjoy!

Enjoy
decon
struc
latte
nitro
coffee

y my
n-
ted
or
e.

CHISUM

Bruce

NEXT STOP, THE MOON

Bruce is a totally self-made man with a heart of gold. He made a fortune in the technology sector and likes to flaunt it. He regularly has extra business seats to spare at Yankee Stadium and when he does, I'm invited. Thanks to Bruce, I also get a chance to follow the NBA playoffs in Madison Square Garden from the front row. Before the game, we often have a drink at a rooftop bar in the neighborhood. After that, it's a good steak at the restaurant adjacent to Madison Square Garden. Following dinner, you can ease into the arena via the restaurant without having to line up with hordes of fans pushing through the main entrance. That's a useful tip I also got from a local.

And here's another one: if you want to keep up with a party of successful businessmen, check your bank account first. Since Bruce paid for the food, out of gratitude and kindness I said the beer during the game would be on me. Alas, this doesn't come

cheap in VIP boxes. And since the boys can really booze it up – and also have expensive taste – it ended up costing me as much as the average business seat. Call it a learning experience. But they were welcome to it and I also had a hell of a time.

For Bruce, only the best is good enough. You can tell by how he looks, by his apartment, his country house ... and by what ends up on his plate. The thought of the $25 he once paid for three morsels of cheese in a French restaurant still knocks me over. In The Palm, one of the city's best steakhouses, Bruce, being a loyal customer (think: big spender), was honored by having his caricature added to the Wall of Fame. In time-honored tradition, he was placed among the exclusive club of celebrities, luminaries, and regular customers, which is a fact Bruce is extremely proud of. If you've got it, flaunt it.

Although we've lost touch the last few years, I still have vivid memories of Bruce and I will always remain grateful to him. As a tour guide, every day I help my compatriots grow into New Yorkers. What I do for them now, Bruce did for me then. He took it upon himself to initiate me into American culture. I got my first baseball cap from him. Though I never wore a cap in Belgium, it has become my trademark here. I even have them personalized with a Belgian touch. Because in New York you show pride in your roots. No point in denying it.

A Tip from Bruce

THE PALM
837 2nd Ave.
www.thepalm.com

This steakhouse, run by an Italian family, should actually have been called Parma, after their place of origin. But, due to their heavy Italian accent, the registration bureau clerk misheard the name and it became "The Palm" instead of "The Parma." The tradition of caricatures on the wall started long ago as an alternative payment method for the destitute artists who came there to eat.

New York Stadiums

YANKEE STADIUM
1 E 161st St, Bronx, NY 10451
newyork.yankees.mlb.com/nyy/ballpark

The home of the New York Yankees is (at $1.5 billion) the second most expensive stadium in the world. After each game the loudspeakers belt out "New York, New York". In the early days, when the Yankees won, Frank Sinatra's widely-known cover would be played; when they lost it would be Liza Minnelli's original film version. That is, until Ms. Minnelli expressed her dissatisfaction. Now only Sinatra's version is played, whatever the score.

NEW YORK

YANKEES

NEW YORK

MADISON SQUARE GARDEN
4 Penn Plaza
www.thegarden.com

Madison Square Garden sounds familiar to most ears. It's one of the world's busiest multifunctional arenas and presents numerous concerts, shows, and sporting events. It is also home to the New York Rangers, New York Knicks, and New York Liberty. Since 1968, this event venue has been located above Pennsylvania Station (Penn Station for short), between 31st and 33rd Streets and 7th and 8th Avenues. Not Madison Avenue, as the stadium's name might suggest. The name comes from the arena's previous location on Madison Square.

CITI FIELD
123-01 Roosevelt Ave.
Flushing, Queens
newyork.mets.mlb.com/nym/ballpark

Citi Field (named after the financial giant Citigroup) is the New York Mets' home base and is located in Queens, just next to the US Open Tennis Complex. For a long time the imposing structure's dimensions were a detriment to the sport. The high wall surrounding the outfield literally got in the way of homeruns, causing the team always to end up last in their category. To help out the Mets, it was decided to cut the wall in half.

BARCLAYS CENTER
620 Atlantic Ave., Brooklyn
www.barclayscenter.com

It has a long history behind it, but these days the Barclays Center struts its stuff on Atlantic Avenue in Brooklyn. "Masters of the house" are the Brooklyn Nets although, as well as being a basketball arena, the center also serves as a multifunctional event

---

FUN FACT

There is some dispute about the origin of the word Yankee but a recurring and plausible theory is that it comes from the popular Dutch name Jan-Kees (pronounced yan-case).

venue. In 2012 Jay Z had the honor of being the first to perform there. The fact that he was one of the Barclays Center's investors *and* helped design the Nets' logo may have a little something to do with this.

METLIFE STADIUM

I MetLife Stadium Dr., East Rutherford, NJ 07073
www.metlifestadium.com
Although located in New Jersey, the MetLife Stadium, the most expensive stadium ever built, often sees the New York Jets and the New York Giants competing on its turf. For the sweet sum of $1.6 billion, the fans were treated to 80,000 seats. Since two teams share the complex, it is lit at night in different colors: green for the Jets and blue for the Giants.

SEASONS

NFL
FOOTBALL SEASON

SEPTEMBER — FEBRUARY

NBA
BASKETBALL SEASON

OCTOBER — MAY

MAJOR LEAGUE
BASEBALL SEASON

MARCH — SEPTEMBER

NHL
HOCKEY SEASON

OCTOBER — JUNE

FUN FACT
They don't penny-pinch when it comes to sports in New York. All its stadiums, costing at least a billion dollars each, are in the top 10 of the world's most expensive venues.

Mmmmm-burgers

You can get a hamburger everywhere. They're available in all shapes and sizes and vary in price from one dollar to several hundred. But which is the best? There are about as many opinions on this as there are people in New York. Still, here are a few tips.

SHAKE SHACK

www.shakeshack.com

As far as major chains are concerned, Shake Shack is by far the best choice. What started out as a hotdog stand quickly grew into an immensely popular hamburger chain (that owes its name to the tasty milkshakes). Shake Shack even won the "Best Burger" Award. Now, it's an international company with ten branches in New York City alone. The first milkshake shack is still there in Madison Square Park, right where it all began. Just look for the longest line. You can't miss it.

BAREBURGER

www.bareburger.com

This burger joint does its best to use only organic and natural ingredients and you can taste it. Fair trade, pesticide-free and free range are basic principles here. Bareburger also serves vegetarian and gluten-free meals. Their efforts produce tasty dishes and a well-deserved special mention.

SPOTTED PIG

314 West 11th Street

www.thespottedpig.com

Judging by the place's relaxed atmosphere, it may not be immediately obvious but The Spotted

Pig has an honor roll with a capital H. Notables such as Bill Clinton, Jay Z, Beyoncé, Michael Stipe, and Kanye West are regular customers. Evidently, they want to enjoy good food at an agreeable price too. The hamburgers here are professionally grilled and served on homemade buns with delicious Roquefort cheese. Bon appétit.

EXPENSIVE TASTE

For a while, Serendipity 3, a restaurant on the Upper East Side, was selling the world's most expensive hamburger. For just under $300 you could gorge on

Le Burger Extravagant, complete with truffles and edible gold. "We can do that," thought the guys from Food Truck 666. They even took it up a notch and created the Douche Burger. This burger also contains 24 karat gold and goes for a reasonable $666. In addition, it includes every conceivable costly ingredient. That means *foie gras*, caviar, lobster, cheese melted in champagne steam, and Himalayan salt. It comes neatly wrapped in genuine $100 bills. The question is whether it's any good. It was a devilishly good idea, in any case. Sales of their regular burgers ($6.66) have skyrocketed since the launch of the Douche Burger.

Allison

UNDER ONE ROOF

In the first weeks of my New York adventure it quickly became clear to me that finding affordable accommodation in New York can be frustrating. Cramped quarters for sizable sums are the norm here. To give you an idea: the going price for a studio in Manhattan is over $2,000 a month. To cut costs, I was forced to sublet a room in the apartment I was renting from my then employer, Israel Katz, the owner of Jardin Bistro in SoHo. That's how I met Allison. She responded to my Craigslist ad and became my first roommate and girlfriend in New York City.

I could have done worse. You never know what you're getting with a new roomie and even though it's preceded by an interview, you only really get to know someone well after having shared a place with them for a while. Especially when you're living cheek by jowl, which is almost always the case in New York's overcrowded dwellings. I still vividly remember finding a portion of Allison's wardrobe in the refrigerator. "Every space has to be utilized," she said, "my closet is too small." And, you bet, I even found her clothes in the freezer. It isn't only an alternative storage space, it also kills germs and saves you a trip to the laundromat, she reasoned. Saving space *and* money? I couldn't argue with that.

Allison turned out to be not only an asset to my social life but also a talented photographer. At one point, she was commissioned to photograph a new park, the High Line. Once a railroad track, this unique display of fine landscape architecture cuts right through the Chelsea neighborhood. On the south side, the green zone passes under the Standard Hotel and from Allison's pictures we discovered that, from up on the High Line, more hotel room activities could be seen than prudish Americans would deem proper. The hotel was, for a while, a subject of scandal and a favored spot for exhibitionist couples. Today, guests booking a room at the Standard may find themselves asked to show some discretion.

After we parted ways, Allison prospered. Her photos were placed on the cover of the New York Times. Her fundraising project for a group of underprivileged girls who are part of a surf club in Bangladesh went viral and raised $21,000, much more than the requested $9,000. She has no fewer than 30,000 followers on Instagram. Congratulations, Allison. I am very proud and happy to have shared a place with such a philanthropist. (bangladeshsurfing.com)

A Tip from Allison

B&H
420 9th Ave., corner of West 34th St.
www.bhphotovideo.com

Never buy electrical appliances in any of the myriad tourist shops on Times Square. For better prices, quality, and warranties you'd be better off in one of the specialized stores, such as B&H. This electronics factory, run more or less solely by orthodox Jews, is worth a visit in any case if for no other reason than to get a closer look at its proficient organization or the intricate network of conveyor belts on the ceiling.

Living in New York

Unless you're swimming in money, you don't live spaciously in New York. The rents here are as high as the buildings. A studio in Midtown Manhattan could easily cost you $2,500 a month. A two-bedroom apartment could go right up to $4,000. So it's no surprise that, to lower costs, most New Yorkers live with one or more roommates. The search for an acceptable abode in this city is, in itself, a major adventure. Everyone's got a story about uninhabitable hovels, deranged roommates, impossible neighbors, or negligent landlords. Living in cramped quarters means having to make do with a kitchenette or even no kitchen at all and room for a washing machine is completely out of the question. Consequently, New Yorkers hardly ever cook. And it isn't even less expensive than takeout or ordering online. The laundry problem is solved by the hundreds of laundromats in town and many residences have similar laundry rooms in their basements. So be prepared to downsize your expectations if you're thinking of moving to New York. Here, the luxury, space, and peace you take for granted at home is strictly for the *happy few* with a very above-average income.

Craigslist

Less familiar to my fellow Continentals, Craigslist (.org) is *the* website for classifieds. Despite its retro 90's design, this site still draws more than 60 million users a month. All those surfers provide an enormous supply of jobs, rooms and apartments, goods, services, and a generous dose of hopeful singles. This list was initially created by programmer Craig Newmark to help his friends stay up to speed on the goings-on in the San Francisco area. Now, Craigslist has become a household name as well as a useful tool for anyone looking for or offering anything.

A Tip from Patrick

Even more so than Craigslist, websites such as Airbnb have become tremendously popular among visitors searching for temporary lodgings. Although these new resources offer many advantages, a certain degree of caution is recommended. I occasionally hear stories from clients about things going wrong. For example, booking a stay at an address that turns out to be nonexistent when they get there. So be on your guard before making that deposit.

Top photo spots in New York

TOP OF THE ROCK
Rockefeller Center, 45 Rockefeller Plaza
Between 49th and 50th St. and 5th and 6th Ave.

For a breathtaking 360° panorama of the city, go to the top of the General Electric Building in Rockefeller Center. The view is awesome and a photographer could really have a ball there. The view of the city is unobstructed, unlike at the top of the Empire State Building, with its annoying grillwork. You're best off going there just before sunset. That way, you can still enjoy the magnificent view in daylight, the setting sun, and the innumerable New York lights after it gets dark. Get your index finger into shape.

EAST RIVER

The East River provides the best view of the Manhattan skyline on the eastside. Always carry a watch because you can easily lose track of time in the following places.
- **FDR Four Freedoms Park, the southernmost point of Roosevelt Island.**
- **Gantry Plaza State Park, 4-09 47th Road, Long Island City.**
- **Northside Piers, North Williamsburg, Brooklyn.**

BROOKLYN BRIDGE PARK
Pier I, Brooklyn

The Lower Manhattan skyline is also jaw-droppingly stunning material. The financial district boasts showpiece architecture and, along with the Brooklyn Bridge, it is one of the most photogenic spots in all of New York City. Do yourself a favor and pack an extra memory card.

THE HIGH LINE
Van Gansevoort St. to 34th St.

This promenade abounds with spots where architecture and nature combine to form stunning tableaus. Besides esthetically correct walks, thanks to its geographical elevation this park provides a unique perspective of the city. From Instagrammer to professional photographer; there's something here for everyone.

194

STARBUCKS

83

Manhattan is the only urban area in the US with more Starbucks than McDonald's.

MCDONALD'S

FROM YUPPIE TO HIPSTER

DOWNTOWN FIDI TO WILLIAMSBURG

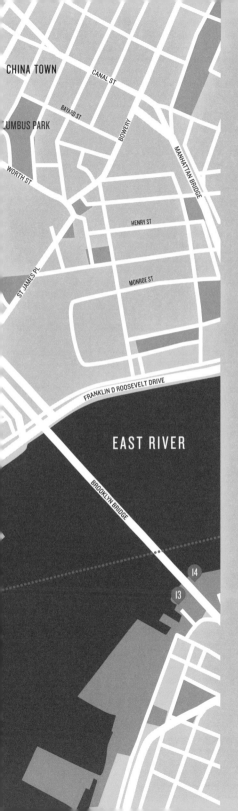

FROM YUPPIE
TO HIPSTER

DOWNTOWN FIDI TO WILLIAMSBURG

 4 TO 5 HOURS   MAP I

1. NEW YORK CITY HALL
2. THE WOOLWORTH BUILDING
3. THE SEPTEMBER II MEMORIAL
4. OCULUS
5. TRINITY CHURCH
6. NEW YORK STOCK EXCHANGE
7. THE CHARGING BULL
8. THE NATIONAL MUSEUM OF THE AMERICAN INDIAN
9. STONE STREET
10. STATEN ISLAND FERRY
11. PIER II / WALL ST. HELINY
12. HELINY
13. THE RIVER CAFÉ
14. JANE'S CAROUSEL

FROM YUPPIE TO HIPSTER

DOWNTOWN FIDI TO WILLIAMSBURG

MAP 2

15 WALLABOUT BAY
16 GRAND FERRY PARK
17 DOMINO SUGAR FACTORY
18 FREEHOLD
19 MISS FAVELA
20 MARLOW & SONS
21 PETER LUGER STEAK HOUSE
22 VIDEOLOGY
23 BROOKLYN ART LIBRARY -SKETCHBOOK PROJECT
24 MAST BROTHERS CHOCOLATE
25 BLUE BOTTLE COFFEE
26 CAPRICES BY SOPHIE
27 URBAN OUTFITTERS
28 BAGELSMITH BEDFORD
29 McCARREN HOTEL AND POOL
30 BROOKLYN BREWERY
31 WESTLIGHT
32 BROOKLYN BOWL
33 WYTHE HOTEL
34 SPRITZENHAUS
35 FIVE LEAVES
36 LOREN CRONK

On this walk, you take the boat from *yuppie central* to *hipsterville*. Along the way the surroundings gradually change from Stock Exchange and banks to creative concept stores via three monumental bridges. Both the financial district and the trendy Williamsburg are unique areas with their own singular characters. Get ready for an extensive adventure where you will need more of everything: eyes, time, money, and hunger.

❶ NEW YORK CITY HALL
City Hall Park
www.nyc.gov
🕒 Mo.-Fr. 9 a.m.-5 p.m.

The tour begins at the mayor's office. Originally, this town hall dating from 1812 had only a marble facade because it was on the outskirts of a town that would never expand. This turned out to be a miscalculation. The building ended up being too small and the municipal services moved across the road to the bigger, more majestic Municipal Building at 1 Centre Street.

❷ THE WOOLWORTH BUILDING
233 Broadway, between Park Pl. and Barclay St.

One hundred years ago, this 790,000 foot high cathedral of commerce was the tallest building in the world. For $13.5 million, Mr. Woolworth became the owner of this magnificent neo-Gothic specimen. He made his fortune from five and dime stores, which sold inexpensive household items.

❸ THE SEPTEMBER II MEMORIAL
Between Liberty St. and Fulton St., West St. and Greenwich St.
www.911memorial.org

The names of the nearly 3,000 victims of the 9/11 terrorist attacks are engraved in the parapet encircling the two waterfalls where the Twin Towers once stood. Entrance is free to the world's most expensive monument. There's also a museum but you have to pay for that. The Survivor Tree in the park survived the havoc and is a living symbol of America's resilience.

❹ OCULUS
185 Greenwich Street, Manhattan
www.westfield.com/westfieldworld-tradecenter
🕒 Su.-Fr. 10 a.m.-9 p.m.,
Sa. 11 a.m.-7 p.m.

This is the most expensive station on the planet and was designed by Santiago Calatrava. It was supposed to be ready in 2009 and had a budget of $2 billion. Since it was not finished until 2016 and cost twice

as much as planned, it was wisely decided to forgo the grand opening. There's a hole in the hall's roof, which allows daylight to reach down to the platforms. Every September 11, the sun shines through the hole at precisely 10:28 a.m. – the exact moment the second tower collapsed on 9/11.

❺ TRINITY CHURCH
74 Trinity Pl., facing Wall St.
www.trinitywallstreet.org
🕒 Mo.-Fr. 7 a.m.-6 p.m.,
Sa. 10 a.m.-4 p.m., Su. 7 a.m.-4 p.m.

The first church burned down, the second succumbed to bad weather. Trinity Church thus lives up to its name. When Manhattan's richest church was still the city's highest point it also served as a beacon.

❻ NEW YORK STOCK EXCHANGE
11 Wall St.
www.nyse.com

Considering all the crashes and crises the Stock Exchange has weathered, it still looks surprisingly good.

Unfortunately, since 9/11, you aren't allowed to go in and see how the world gets gambled away.

⑦ THE CHARGING BULL

Broadway, at Bowling Green
www.chargingbull.com

The bull was a reaction to the recession of the 1980s. Arturo Di Modica deposited the statue in front of the Exchange in the middle of the night, as a Christmas present to New York. The bronze beast, heavily built at 3.5 tons, proves that not all that glitters is gold. Even so, masses of tourists look for financial bliss here.

⑧ THE NATIONAL MUSEUM OF THE AMERICAN INDIAN

I Bowling Green
nmai.si.edu
◷ Mo.-We. and Fr.-Su. 10 a.m.-5 p.m., Th. 10 a.m.-8 p.m.

This is where Fort Amsterdam once stood, the center of New Amsterdam under Peter Stuyvesant. The current building was, for many years, the customs post for all goods entering the US. Today, it houses all the Indian artifacts collected by George Gustav Heye on his travels in South, Central and North America.

⑨ STONE STREET

Between S William St. and Pearl St.

At 4 p.m. the suits pour out of the financial towers. They often set off for Stone Street, a picturesque alley paved with Belgian blocks. Ideal for a post-business babble, for watching sports, or just for a drink.

⑩ STATEN ISLAND FERRY

Peter Minuit Plaza, Whitehall St.
www.siferry.com
◷ 24/24, 7/7. Every half hour; every hour at night. Mo.-Fr. every 20 mins. at peak times, every 15 mins. during rush hour.

The ferry to Staten Island, the city's forgotten quarter, is also free (this may strengthen your illusion that New York is cheap!). There isn't much to see there, but the voyage offers a nice view of the Statue of Liberty *and* the Downtown Manhattan skyline. If you time it right, the return journey will be after dark, giving you the same panoramas by night.

⑪ PIER II / WALL ST. HELINY

East River Ferry
www.eastriverferry.com
◷ Mo.-Fr. every half hour, every 20 mins. during rush hour, Sa.-Su., every 45 min. Ferry times vary so check the website

⑫ HELINY

Heliport Pier 6
www.heliny.com
◷ Mo.-Su. 9 a.m.-5 p.m.

From here, go to the heliport for an amazing bird's-eye view of New York, or to the landing for a breathtaking nautical tour of Manhattan. To resume the walking tour, take the East River Ferry from Pier 11 to Midtown and get off at Williamsburg North.

⑬ THE RIVER CAFÉ

I Water St.
www.rivercafe.com
◷ Ma.-zo. 17.30-24.00 u

The water taxi's first stop is DUMBO: This is the area in Brooklyn between the Manhattan and the Brooklyn Bridges. You can treat your taste buds at the cozy River Café, under the Brooklyn Bridge's tower. If your date doesn't resemble their picture, there's always the unbeatable panorama of the skyscrapers on which to feast your eyes.

⑭ JANE'S CAROUSEL

Brooklyn Bridge Park
www.janescarousel.com
◷ Mid-May to Sep. We.-Mo. 11 a.m.-7 p.m., Oct. to mid-May Th.-Su.11 a.m.-6 p.m.

This magnificent merry-go-round dating from the early 1920s has been minutely restored. Thanks to the painstaking work, the carousel has been turning again since 2011. For $2 you can hop on for a ride. Hurricane Sandy brought the water up to its windows but the whirligig escaped renewed renovation by a hairsbreadth.

⑮ WALLABOUT BAY

Sounds almost Australian, but this bay owes its name to the Walloons, the French-speaking Belgians, who settled there.

⑯ GRAND FERRY PARK

End of Grand St. at East River

This cute little park was a mooring for the steam ferry. It's tucked away between the factories but your search for it will be rewarded with magnificent views of the Williamsburg Bridge and Manhattan.

⑰ DOMINO SUGAR FACTORY

Kent Ave. and S 1st St.

This old sugar factory once accounted for half of US sugar production. When renovation is completed, this preserved complex will form part of a new construction project including 2,300 apartments, offices, and parks.

⑱ FREEHOLD

45 S 3rd St.
www.freeholdbrooklyn.com
🕐 Su.-We. 7 a.m.-2 a.m.,
Th.-Sa. 7 a.m.-4 a.m.

Time for coffee, cake, and Facebook in this trendy, bright, and airy cafe. But don't linger, there's lots more to discover.

⑲ MISS FAVELA

57 S 5th St.
www.missfavela.com
🕐 Mo.-Su. noon- midnight

Angela Denneulin, wife of a restaurant owner from SoHo, wanted to do her own thing so she opened Miss Favela: a Brazilian bistro serving an exotic brunch. On Sundays there are cocktails, Brazilian beats, and the inevitable swirling of feet.

⑳ MARLOW & SONS

81 Broadway, corner of Berry St.
www.marlowandsons.com
🕐 Mo.-Su. 8 a.m.-4 p.m. and 5 p.m.-midnight

Cool haute cuisine in a canteen. Did you expect anything else from Williamsburg? There is no menu because the food changes every day. The day's dishes are written on the paper table "cloths".

㉑ PETER LUGER STEAK HOUSE

178 Broadway, corner of Driggs Ave.
www.peterluger.com
🕐 Mo.-Th. 11:30 a.m.-9:30 p.m.,
Fr.-Sa. 11:30 a.m.-10:30 p.m.,
Su. 12:30 p.m.-9:30 p.m.

Juicy steaks and full glasses. You won't leave hungry, but possibly dead tired from washing dishes if you forgot they don't accept credit cards here.

㉒ VIDEOLOGY

308 Bedford Ave.
www.videology.info
🕐 Su.-Th. noon-2 a.m., Fr.-Sa. noon-4 a.m.

This three-in-one video rental store, movie theater, and bar is a godsend for all film lovers. There's always something going on, often for free, such as TV series marathons and movie quizzes. There's popcorn too. Check the calendar on their website.

㉓ BROOKLYN ART LIBRARY -SKETCHBOOK PROJECT

28 Frost St., Brooklyn
www.sketchbookproject.com
🕐 Mo.-Su. noon-6 p.m.

Everyone can give their creativity free rein in this art project. For the price of a book you can become part of the collection and share your artistic creations with the world.

㉔ MAST BROTHERS CHOCOLATE

111 N 3rd St., between Wythe Ave. and Berry St.

mastbrothers.co.uk/pages/brooklyn

🕐 Mo.-Sa. 11 a.m.-7 p.m.,

Su. 11 a.m.-5 p.m.

Nothing beats Belgian chocolate, but this comes pretty close. The Mast brothers turned their hobby into a profession and transformed this old building into a trendy chocolate factory. Eat that, Willy Wonka!

㉕ BLUE BOTTLE COFFEE

160 Berry St. between N 4th and 5th St.

www.bluebottlecoffee.com

🕐 Mo.-Th. 7 a.m.-7 p.m.,

Fr.-Su. 7 a.m.-8 p.m.

This coffee roaster on Berry Street serves as a canvas for a work of art by the Belgian artist ROA. The coffee served is roasted and ground on the premises, in line with the demands of the New York caffeine culture. Latte art is more than just an image on your coffee's foam!

㉖ CAPRICES BY SOPHIE

138 N 6th St., between Berry and Bedford St.

www.capricesbysophie.com

🕐 Mo.-Su. 7:30 a.m.-8 p.m.

Sophie left her job in Paris' financial world to turn her hobby into a profession, as I did. I became a guide, she became a baker. And she really takes the cake! That Sophie is still alive is a miracle because her meringues and éclairs are to die for. Everything is made with fresh, locally produced and organic ingredients.

㉗ URBAN OUTFITTERS

89 N 6th St., between Wythe and Berry St.

www.spaceninety8.com

🕐 Mo.-Su. 10 a.m.-10 p.m.

Like everything in this neighborhood, Urban Outfitters is a concept store too. Completely in (clothing) line with the Williamsburgers' expectations of craftsmanship, priority in Space Ninety 8 is given to local designers.

㉘ BAGELSMITH BEDFORD

189 Bedford Ave., between 6th and 7th St.

www.bagelsmith.com

🕐 Open 24/24, 7/7

The best bagels in the area and around the clock too. If you're not hungry yet, buy one for the hunger to come.

㉙ McCARREN HOTEL & POOL

160 North 12th Street

www.mccarrenhotel.com

🕐 Rooftop. We.-Sa. 5 p.m.-4 a.m., Su. 5 p.m.-2 p.m.

The swimming pool, the view, the service, the style... reasons aplenty for a stay at the McCarren Hotel. See you on the roof for a summer party with DJs and cocktails.

㉚ BROOKLYN BREWERY

79 N 11th St.

www.brooklynbrewery.com

🕐 Visits Fr. 6 p.m.-11 p.m., Sa. noon-8 p.m., Su. noon-6 p.m., Mo.-Th. 5 p.m. with reservation and $10 fee.

The sales and the popularity of these Brooklyn beers are constantly on the rise. Lines often start an hour before opening. Be on time!

㉛ WESTLIGHT

The William Vale Hotel, 111 N 12th St, Brooklyn

Westlightnyc.com

🕐 Su.-We. 4 p.m.-midnight, Th.-Sa. 4 p.m.-2 a.m.

In a constantly changing city like New York, there's always the risk of getting ahead of yourself. So permit me this audacity: This is the latest, newest, and best rooftop ever. Take it from me. From up here you can admire Downtown and Midtown Manhattan and see as far as the Bronx. Simply spectacular. Just do it!

32 BROOKLYN BOWL

61 Wythe Ave., between N 11th and 12th St.
www.brooklynbowl.com
Mo.- Fr. 6 p.m.- close,
Sa.- Su. 11 a.m. - close

This is not your run-of-the-mill bowling alley. You're still in Williamsburg; even bowling here is done *hipster style*. The options are: a good concert, a fun evening of bowling, or both at the same time. A bit on the pricey side but guaranteed fun. The food is prepared by Blue Ribbon; apparently these businesses are joined at the hip(ster).

33 WYTHE HOTEL

80 Wythe Avenue, between N 11th and 12th St.
www.wythehotel.com

Converted factories are the hipster's natural habitat. To their great delight, Jed Walentas (son of Jane's Carousel, remember?) turned the old cooperage lock, stock and barrel into the Wythe Hotel. The result appeals to many, bearded and otherwise. Includes a movie theater, restaurant, and roof garden.

34 SPRITZENHAUS

Nassau Ave., between Guernsey and Dobbin St.
www.spritzenhaus33.com
Mo.-We. 4 p.m.-4 a.m.,
Th.-Su. noon-4 a.m.

Spritzenhaus means Belgian fries, sausage with sauerkraut, and a long beer list in a spacious, industrial loft with enormous garage-door-style windows that are raised in the summer, and a burning fire in the winter. What more do you need?

35 FIVE LEAVES

18 Bedford Ave., corner of Lorimer St.
www.fiveleavesny.com
Mo.-Su. 8 a.m.-1 a.m.

Movie star Heath Ledger planned this bistro with a few friends. After he passed away, his family helped realize the plan. Food with an Australian touch in a maritime decor.

36 LOREN CRONK

80 Nassau Ave., between Lorimer St. and Manhattan Ave.
www.lorencronk.com
Mo., We., and Th. noon-7 p.m.,
Fr. noon-9 p.m., Sa.-Su. 11 a.m.-8 p.m.,
Tu. closed.

Making jeans is obviously in Loren's genes. He taught himself the art and opened this charming boutique. Absolute craftsmanship at affordable prices.

SHAY

PARTNERS IN CRIME

Hipster, on the wacky side, incredible, unpredictable, and a hell of a guy. That's Shay in a nutshell. He made the transition from Tel Aviv lawyer to sandwich bar owner in the center of New York. Not because it was his life's dream, but because after a few footloose years it was time to make a living. "Might as well sell hummus," he thought, and opened The Picnic Basket in the fashion district, near Macy's. With a good plan, some luck, and all his connections in "Jew York", he hit the jackpot. It was such a success that he quickly opened a second branch.

Shay is a survivor. He knows his way around New York and is never short of an impressive feat. When he broke his wrist he drove himself to the hospital. Because it saved money. And to prevent his electricity from being cut off, he pretended, on the phone to the energy supplier, to be a confused old lady. Spur of the moment, but it worked.

His impulsive character will literally always be with him. He had his favorite T-shirt's design tattooed on his chest. Of course, the next day he called me to tell me he regretted it.

With Shay there's always an adventure brewing. We often go exploring together. His connections and knowledge of New York have taken me to plenty of unexpected places. There's nothing more fun for a tour guide than discovering new things in the city you've fallen in love with. Since the success of the first edition of this book and his well-received appearance on a Belgian TV show, I can always count on him to guide a few groups. That way, more people can reap the benefits of all that passion.

© Adrian Gaut

A TIP FROM PATRICK

A TIP FROM SHAY

WYTHE HOTEL

80 Wythe Ave. North 11th St.,
Williamsburg, Brooklyn
www.wythehotel.com

The Wythe Hotel offers a skyline
view with a capital S (and V). This
dilapidated factory in the facelifted
Williamsburg was converted into a 72-
room stylish hotel, the farm-to-table
restaurant Reynard, and the trendy
rooftop bar The Ides. It even has its
own screening room with adjacent bar
for movies and presentations.
www.reynardnyc.com
www.wythehotel.com/the-ides

MCCARREN HOTEL & POOL

160 North 12th St., Williamsburg, Brooklyn
www.mccarrenhotel.com

Not far from the Wythe Hotel lies the McCarren
Hotel, which provides not only a view equally
as beautiful as the Wythe's, but also one of
Brooklyn's largest open-air salt-water pools.
Considering the price, a swim there could be
termed luxurious, though not a luxury during the
hot summer months.

MCCARREN PARK POOL

N. 12 St., Lorimer St., Manhattan Ave., between Bayard
St. and Berry St.
www.nycgovparks.org/parks/mccarrenpark/facilities/
outdoor-pools/mccarren-park-pool

If a swim at the McCarren Hotel doesn't fit your
budget, you could always take a dip across the
street. The McCarren Park's open-air Olympic-
size swimming pool offers free admission during
the summer months. No towel service here, of
course. Also bring a lock for your locker.

JEW YORK CITY

The source of this epithet is no mystery. There are more than one million Jews in the Greater New York City Area. This is more than the combined Jewish population of Boston, Philadelphia, Chicago, San Francisco, and Washington. It is the largest Jewish community in the world. Excluding Israel, of course.

ART GALLERIES

Not only does New York have a multitude of galleries, each year the city is inundated with renowned art fairs, of which Frieze and The Armory Show are by far the most famous. The reason is simple: anyone who can spare a couple of million for an apartment wouldn't bat an eye at spending a couple of thousand to decorate their imitation mantelpiece. But it can also come cheaper. When the British street artist Banksy was in New York in 2013, he spent a day selling his work on the street. At the end of the day, only a handful of unsuspecting passersby had bought a $60 canvas – more than 300 times less than their actual worth. Better still: One old lady managed to wheedle out a 50% discount and expected a free plastic bag, too.

A TIP FROM PATRICK

Chelsea has now built quite a name for itself when it comes to galleries and exhibition rooms. You practically stumble over them in this neighborhood, especially between 10th and 11th Avenues and 18th and 28th Streets. At their peak, they numbered around 350, of which some 200 still exist. You wouldn't exactly call it a great loss; it's more that the neighborhood has matured. These days, however, another neighborhood is attracting attention again. Specifically, the Lower East Side, where the art scene is regenerating after having to relocate to the then cheaper Chelsea in the 1980s. The last few years have seen the opposite trend, although both neighborhoods still retain their own special character..

ISRAEL

I MISS THE OLD NEW YORK

I was pretty hard up when I first arrived in New York. I had only just enough to rent a room in Brooklyn. There was no way I could afford extra luxuries such as bedclothes, so my Burberry jacket had to fulfill that function for a while. Finding work was literally a matter of life or death.

For Craigslist, see Allison's profile

I scoured all the Belgian restaurants in vain and eventually, via a Craigslist ad, found Israel Katz, owner of Le Jardin Bistro. This French restaurant on Petrosino Square was very successful in the 1980s and 90s but by now it was past its prime. My knowledge of French would renew his business' cachet. So Israel gave me my first job and my first apartment. With the help of some paint and linoleum, the run-down apartment in Chinatown I rented from him was turned into what could just barely be defined as acceptable accommodation. The neighbors' daily "refreshed" smell of fish was part of the deal.

FABBRICA
40 N 6th St.,
Williamsburg

Israel often expressed his dissatisfaction about the disappearance of the real New York, which was being replaced by the corporate world's big chains. To reinforce his sentiments, being the eccentric that he is, he had "I miss the old New York" tattooed on his arm. Oh, the bygone days of yore. With a Duane Reade or a Starbucks on every corner, he'd had it with Manhattan and moved to trendy Williamsburg in Brooklyn, where he started running the Fabbrica restaurant. Following the publication of the first edition of this book in 2014, I understand he was very frequently visited by well-to-do ladies on girls' city trips. Ladies, I'm sorry to say that comely Katz beat it. Fabbrica still exists but has been sold. Israel exchanged his carefree existence for a considerably responsible job at Houston airport. Still determined to see him? Food & Beverage department. You didn't get it from me.

A FEW TIPS
FROM ISRAEL

ROSEMARY'S GREENPOINT TAVERN

188 Bedford Ave., Williamsburg, Brooklyn, between North 6th and 7th

This is an unpretentious, old-school cafe with corresponding prices. If you're in the mood for an affordable beer (in a plastic glass) in the company of locals, rockers, and other musicians, then Rosemary's is the place. Be patient with the bartenders; they're about as old as the school.

DECIBEL

240 East 9th St., between Stuyvesant St. and 2nd Ave.

www.sakebardecibel.com

For more than twenty years Decibel has been serving authentic Japanese rice wine in a variety of types, numbering almost a hundred. You could call it a sake speakeasy, since the bar is literally underground. There isn't much more than a small sign to indicate the entrance. Through the iron gate and down the stairs, then step right into Japan. Kanpai!

A TIP FROM PATRICK

BARCADE
388 Union Ave., Williamsburg, Brooklyn
www.barcadebrooklyn.com

A few cold beers and a large collection of old video games were the recipe for many fun evenings for two brothers and their friends. It wasn't too long before the idea came about to commercialize this concept. The four of them moved the old machines from a loft to a former metal store in a warehouse in Williamsburg. It was such a success that they subsequently opened three more branches. A must-"play" for lovers of computer games from the 1980s.

DUANE READE

This drugstore is a Manhattan monument. Every day it serves no fewer than 300,000 New Yorkers. The chain takes its name from the location of the first store between Duane Street and Reade Street and owes its success to the fact that it completely gets New Yorkers. A New Yorker isn't fazed by narrow corridors or staircases. What matters is supply and speed. Aware of this fact, Duane Reade audaciously places its stores in small, narrow, storied buildings; something no other supermarket would ever dare. No shortage of cashiers: The client doesn't have time to wait. Its merchandise also provides a clue to the city it serves. Duane Reade sells twice as many insoles as its competition's average because it knows that New Yorkers are heavy-duty walkers. No chain store in the US has a contraceptive in its top 50 of items sold. Duane Reade has no fewer than three in its top 25. And Viagra, too. That's what you call life in the fast lane.

SHOES ARE MADE FOR WALKING

SHOES

Since your legs cover many miles, adapted footwear is indispensable. The trick is to find the right balance between comfort and esthetically responsible footgear. Unless you find the combination of a suit and sneakers irresistible, of course. But would you take it to the street?

I MIS

THE

NEW

YORK

S

OLD

K.

ALL THINGS BELGIAN

My origins, as are those of many Americans, lie in the ancient continent of Europe; more specifically in small but sympathetic Belgium. Call me proud, but I must say that anything Belgian is a hit in New York. Besides the usual business of beer and chocolate, Belgian fries, waffles, fashion, music, and art have all conquered their piece of New York. Being a Belgian New Yorker, I can assure you that the addresses on the following page are really special. Does all this get you in a Belgian mood? Then don't wait to go to the world's coziest kingdom! Only six hours from JFK – that's right, less than to LA – and you're in waffle and Stella country. But watch out for those Belgians! They'll gladly let you taste all the beers but will stick to only one sort themselves, thus avoiding the same hangover you'll wake up with the next morning. Brussels Airlines has been flying to Brussels and back since 1947. *Welcome aboard, welkom aan boord, bienvenu à bord!*
www.brusselsairlines.com

BELGIAN RESTAURANTS IN NEW YORK

BXL
BXL Café, 125 West, 43d St., between 6th and Broadway
BXL Zoute, 50 West, 22nd St., between 5th and 6th
www.bxlrestaurants.com

PETITE ABEILLE
44 W 17th St., New York, NY
401 E 20th St., New York, NY
134 W Broadway, New York, NY
www.petiteabeille.com

PAIN QUOTIDIEN
26 different locations all over the city,
including Central Park
www.lepainquotidien.com

MARKT
676 Avenue of the Americas, New York, NY
www.marktrestaurant.com

WAFELS & DINGES CAFE
Avenue B and 2nd St.
www.wafelsanddinges.com

POMMES FRITES
128 Macdougal., New York, NY
www.pommesfritesnyc.com

NEUHAUS
460 Grand Central Terminal
www.neuhauschocolate.com

BELGIAN CONTRIBUTIONS TO THE US

brusselsairlines.com/Belgium-ettes

Belgium is one of the most difficult countries to find on a map. So maybe it's no coincidence that it's a country with an acute shortage of patriotism. I'll leave it to you to decide whether this is a blessing or a curse. What the modest Belgians, however, don't know is that their homeland is present in New York on every street corner, in every jazz bar, and even in every American's wallet. Here are a few samples from the lengthy list of inventions that now form part of the United States' DNA.

SAXOPHONE

There would be no Charlie Parker or John Coltrane without the Belgian instrument maker Adolphe Sax. Developed in 1840s Brussels as an improvement to the bass clarinet, the saxophone was quickly purchased in large numbers by the American Army for their military bands, after the Civil War.

ROLLER SKATES

There would be no Xanadu or Roller Disco without the Belgian inventor John Joseph Merlin. Interesting detail: His first prototype in 1760 was nothing more than an ice skate with wheels instead of a blade – in other words, inline skates. The first model, however, was difficult to steer and

didn't have brakes. After an unimaginable number of accidents resulting in bruised knees, ribs, and jaws the concept was put on hold for at least half a century.

TAPES

The "compact cassette" – that's what it was called back then – was invented by the Belgian Lou Ottens in 1963. Just one year later it flooded the American market and countless talented musicians were forced to search for even smaller hovels due to all the illegal copies being made of their work.

SANTA CLAUS

Always been curious about why Father Christmas is called by the strange name

GO BEYOND CHOCOLATE

of Santa Claus? Again, to find the answer we have to go to Belgium. The Belgian and Dutch children's holiday "Sinterklaas" refers to Saint Nicolas (Sint-Nicolaas) who, on the night of December 5, delivers presents to the houses of all the good children. The Dutch and Belgians who had moved to the budding New Amsterdam brought this saint with them the States.

ASPHALT

There would be no asphalt without Belgium. Historians will assert that the Mesopotamians had already used asphalt to make their baths leak-proof, but it was none other than the Belgian chemist Edward de Smedt who, in 1870, invented the modern asphalt concrete.

To be perfectly honest, he invented it at Columbia University. The first modern asphalt road was laid in Newark.

DOLLAR BILLS

There's a bit of Belgium in every dollar. Since 1962, the Belgian company Vervaeke in Kuurne, West Flanders, has been the exclusive supplier of the flax with which every dollar bill is made. For reasons unknown to us, residents of Kuurne are known as jackasses.

More Belgian inventions that changed the world include the World Wide Web, the Big Bang Theory, the praline, cricket, the body mass index, Imodium, the electric tram and metro, rubber, gypsy swing, the stock exchange, and the intercontinental ballistic missile.

**FUN FACTS
FROM BELGIUM**
Belgium is a country with only 11 million inhabitants. Since the French-speaking and Flemish-speaking populations could never really get along, there are now six different local authorities. So you could say that New York City, with one mayor and one city council presiding over almost 9 million inhabitants from all over the world, is a whole lot more efficient.

**FUN FACTS
FROM BELGIUM**
Belgian men are the second tallest in the world. With an average height of 5.96 feet they are second only to the Dutch at 5.99 feet. The women are only 21st, at 5.43 feet. So that would mean a perfect match for an American man of 5.76 ft. No insinuations, of course.

HEART OF EUROPE

Allow me, a Belgian American, to sing the praises of my small homeland. Belgium is, besides beer country, also the heart of Europe. The perfect base, therefore, for anyone wanting to sip red wine in a Parisian sidewalk cafe in the shadow of the Eiffel Tower or try a joint in an Amsterdam coffee shop. It's less than an hour to the center of Paris and less than two to the centers of London or Amsterdam.
Brussels-Paris and Brussels-Amsterdam:
www.thalys.com
Brussels-London:
www.eurostar.com

VISIT FLANDERS

Flanders has as much to offer New Yorkers pining for their home city as it does to Belgians homesick for the city break of their dreams. If you belong to one of these two categories, try the following spots.

ANTWERP

Belgium's New York; therefore, not surprisingly, my home-town. Europe's first skyscraper was built here. Antwerp is also one of the world's fashion capitals and an international seaport. That's one up for this beautiful city on New York's mini-marina.
www.visitantwerpen.be

PATRICK'S PLACES IN ANTWERP

SJALOT EN SCHANUL
Oude Beurs 12, Antwerp
www.sjalotenschanul.be
Positively Belgian fare; tasty and good. But not only that: this place is the nerve center of the Antwerp LGBT community, which is evident from the rainbow colors on the Statue of Liberty inside. The owners, Marieke and Chrisje, have good reason to be nuts about New York.

MAURICE COFFEE AND KNITS
Schoenmarkt 35, Antwerp
www.mauricecoffeeknits.com
More in the mood for coffee and fashion? In the Boerentoren (farmers' tower) – yep, the first skyscraper on European territory – you'll find Maurice Coffee and Knits, a coffee bar/knitting label founded by the extremely beautiful ex-TV star Veronique Leysen.

GHENT

Among the medieval facades and along the many canals, every day a high-tech future is being built. The people of Ghent are known for their hospitality and joie de vivre. During the Ghent Festival, a great celebration that draws more than one million visitors annually, the whole city is dominated by *sex, drugs, and rock'n'roll* for ten days.
www.visitgent.be

PATRICK'S PLACES IN GHENT

JIGGERS
Oudburg 16, Ghent
www.jiggers.be
Homesick or in the mood for the New York speakeasy feeling? This cocktail bar is on the list of the world's best. You can only get in by ringing the doorbell. The menu is handwritten and the cocktails are perfect – just like the hipster bartenders' coiffures.

DREAMCATCHERS
Schepenhuisstraat 17, Ghent
www.wearedreamcatchers.be
Believe it or not, coffee is drunk here among felines. And, if you like, you can adopt one of the purring protégés. Lana Bauwens, the owner, worked for two years in an animal shelter in New York. If you don't click, you don't adopt; that's one of the things she learned there.

BRUGES

Admittedly, you have to look hard to find a bit of New York here. But a visit to Belgium without seeing Bruges is like going to New York and skipping the Empire State Building. Countless cathedrals, churches, and cloisters. Since 2000 the entire city center has been listed as a World Heritage Site. Do your best to avoid weekends because then the official language is Japanese.
www.visitbruges.be

SANSEVERIA BAGELSALON
Predikherenstraat 11, Bruges
www.sanseveria.be
The people of Bruges know very well that American's can't survive without their bagels. Except that here they are served in an ultra-Flemish decor with corresponding ultra-Flemish service. This is like the typical living room of your Flemish grandmother. Sansevierias on the windowsill and a cuckoo clock on the wall.

CHOCOLATIER DUMON
Simon Stevinplein 11, Bruges
www.chocolatierdumon.be
You can't visit Bruges and not go home with bags full of chocolate. It's difficult to make a choice from the hundreds of praline and chocolate shops but, take it from me, Dumon on the beautiful Stevin Square is the best choice.

VISIT BRUSSELS

Europe's New York? Politically and musically at least. The headquarters of the European Union are here and Brussels was for years the capital of jazz as well. There are still countless jazz festivals held every year. The Galeries Royales Saint-Hubert, near the Central Station, is the world's oldest shopping mall, by the way.
www.visitbrussels.be

PATRICK'S PLACES IN BRUSSELS

CAFÉ BELGA
Eugène Flageyplein 18, Elsene
Cafe Belga, on the amazing Flagey Square, is where you can experience ancient Belgium's unadulterated coziness surrounded by multicultural youth. When the sun shines, beach chairs are spread around the square, with a view of the country's most beautiful city park.

NEUHAUS BOUTIQUE
Koninginnegalerij 25, Brussel
www.neuhauschocolate.com
Godiva, Leonidas, and Neuhaus can all be found in the Galeries Saint-Hubert but, according to historians, Jean Neuhaus was the one who actually developed the praline. This pharmacist's son opened a bakery on this very spot and made his first filled chocolate bonbon here in 1912.

VISIT WALLONIA

Will you be in Belgium over Christmas? Then follow the hordes of Flemings on their way to the French-speaking side of our country. This is where you'll find the pretty Ardennes – closely resembling the Hudson Valley or the Catskills – a wooded area where you can take time out for some delightful hiking.
www.wallonia.be

A TIP FROM PATRICK

SPA
To a New Yorker, the name "Spa" sounds like any random health resort – many would also assume the city is so named due to the fact that it has a health spa. Nope. It's actually the other way round: All the spas in the world owe their name to this town. The therapeutic waters of these hot baths was famous as early as the 16th century. The first health resort was built here in 1764, after which Spa soon became so well-known that from then on every health spa in the world was named after it. European sovereigns, nobility, writers, and composers all had a villa or a castle built here. The castles are still there, the hot baths remain open, and the town is an ideal base for exploring the Ardennes.

The Thermes of Spa
Colinne d'Annette et Lubin, Spa
www.thermesdespa.com

TOM

QUALITY TIME

Tom is a great guy. He's someone you can really rely on and who, considering his success, is still pretty modest. Our bond has only grown stronger with the years and I'm happy to count him as one of my best friends in New York. He and his boyfriend Matt live together in a stylish apartment on the periphery of Gramercy, a neighborhood on Manhattan's Lower East Side. When they're not at their house in the Hamptons, that is. Or their country house in Florida.

A successful lawyer and banker, Tom is a good example of how the well-to-do live in New York. His dog Frazier goes to a hotel every day; when they go out or travel, VIP upgrades are matter of course; and if his watch has to be repaired it can easily cost $500 or more. A pittance for a watch with a five-digit price tag. A present from his boyfriend, he told me. A present that, shortly after receiving, he "hid too well" when they were travelling abroad. Since he didn't dare come home

without it, he bought a new one over there. But he got caught red-wristed: the months displayed on his new watch were in Spanish. He hadn't thought about that when he was buying it.

Thanks to Tom, I got to know the Circle Line Sightseeing Cruises. These cruises are also very popular among New Yorkers. The well-guided three-hour cruise shows you Manhattan in all its glory. Obviously, Tom wanted to experience this from a VIP seat. As a *budget traveler*, I wondered secretly whether the special mug and bonus pillows were worth the extra cost. But the cruise is high quality and that's what interested Tom.

Even with such high quality, there's room for improvement. That's how Tom sees it. He moved from the luxury villa in the Hamptons to an even larger palace on Shelter Island. He's already invited me five times to come and enjoy all that beauty firsthand, but a busy schedule and fatherhood have prevented me from going to unwind with him. Whatever the case, Tom is and always will be my most successful friend.

A FEW TIPS FROM TOM

WESTLIGHT WILLIAM VEAL HOTEL
III North 12th Street, Brooklyn
www.westlightnyc.com
A 360° skyline crowns this magnificent hotel. Here, "hipster chic" blends effortlessly with travelling young Europeans. Looking for romance? This is the place for transatlantic love.

© Peter Sylvester

THE OLD TOWN BAR
45 East 18th St., between Broadway and Park Ave.
www.oldtownbar.com
The Old Town Bar's name is not arbitrary. The pub has been around since 1892 and boasts a rich classic interior of mahogany, marble, and tin. It exudes history. Even the stately porcelain urinals have been providing a service for more than a century.

GRAMERCY TAVERN
42 E 20th St.
www.gramercytavern.com
New York loves this restaurant, which is reputed to be one of the city's best. All that embodies the best of contemporary classic American cuisine can be found here. Not cheap, but topnotch quality. And, of course, this again means reserving well in advance.

A TIP FROM PATRICK

GRAMERCY TERRACE
2 Lexington Ave.
www.gramercyparkhotel.com/events/gramercy_terrace
The top floor of the Gramercy Hotel is a green oasis where, surrounded by tropical plants, you can snugly enjoy a drink or a romantic dinner. In the summer the roof is removed, allowing the sun to add the finishing touch. Pretty pricey but worth every cent. Before you rush to the roof, stop and take a look at the Gramercy Hotel's exceptional art collection. The art exhibited here can easily compete with the average museum. Feast your eyes on masterpieces by bigwigs such as Andy Warhol, Damien Hirst, and Keith Haring.

PEOPLE YOU MAY KNOW WHO HAVE A HOME IN THE HAMPTONS

Alec Baldwin
Anderson Cooper
Billy Joel
Calvin Klein
Donna Karan
Gwyneth Paltrow
Howard Stern
Jennifer Lopez
Jerry Seinfeld
Martha Stewart
Paul McCartney
Paul Simon
Ralph Lauren
Renee Zellweger
Richard Gere
Robert De Niro
Sarah Jessica Parker
Steven Spielberg
Scarlett Johansson

THE HAMPTONS

From Calvin Klein to former mayor Michael Bloomberg. Name any famous person and chances are that they own a country house in the Hamptons. This remote corner of Long Island, a two-hour drive east of New York City, is high society's pre-eminent summer stomping ground. Besides an abundance of golf courses and tennis courts, magnificent nature and tranquility, it includes the country's most expensive real estate. If you want to rub shoulders with the stars, there are two ways to reach the Hamptons: The Cannonball, the nonstop express train from Penn Station, or the Hampton Jitney, a bus line with several stops in Manhattan and Brooklyn.

JITNEY
www.hamptonjitney.com
CANNONBALL
web.mta.info/lirr/hamptons/reserveservice.htm

NEW YORK FROM THE WATER

CIRCLE LINE

The Circle Line offers several high-quality cruises led by guides who are experts in their field. The point of departure is on the Hudson, Manhattan's west bank, at Midtown. The cruise provides a view of the west side of the Manhattan skyline, of New Jersey on the opposite shore, and much more, depending on which tour you take. The Circle Line is the most expensive of the three boat tour options but you definitely get your money's worth. Absolutely worth considering.

EAST RIVER FERRY

The East River Ferry is a great way of getting a good perspective of Manhattan while enjoying a spectacular view. The water taxi departs from 34th Street in Midtown Manhattan, has stops in Queens and Brooklyn, and ends at Pier 11 in Lower Manhattan, near Wall Street and the financial district. En route you navigate under New York's three most renowned bridges (Brooklyn, Manhattan, and Williamsburg). All this costs you only $4 per person. Highly recommended.

STATEN ISLAND FERRY

In terms of a free attraction, this one is terrific. You embark at the southern-most point of Manhattan, at the Staten Island Ferry buildings (you can't miss them) and sail past the Statue of Liberty towards Staten Island. When you get there, you can immediately take the next ferry back. Definitely worth it. If you plan it well, you can ferry over in daylight and back after dark. That way you can enjoy two magnificent panoramas of the city in a single trip.

DOGS IN NEW YORK

Considering the limited living space the average New Yorker has to contend with, the number of pets in the city is striking. More than a million four-legged friends (an estimated 600,000 dogs and 500,000 cats) keep New Yorkers company. They support a flourishing business of pet stores and dog hotels. Wag.com home delivers every conceivable pet necessity, while a professional dog walker will let your dog out for $15 per thirty minutes. So a walker with ten or even twenty dogs in tow is not an unusual sight. An amusing spectacle, definitely a skill, and a lucrative one at that.

FUN FACT
Plenty of pets are on the New York blacklist. Unless your name is Bronx or Brooklyn Zoo, you can't have any poisonous snakes, iguanas, ferrets, squirrels, or ducks. So don't follow the example of Joey from Friends. Believe it or not, one of the animals on the list of forbidden pets is the whale.

MILLION DOLLAR BABIES

Little Blue Ivy Carter had barely drawn her first breath before the cost of her birth was spread over the pages of all the tabloids and papers. Jay Z and Beyoncé paid no less than $1.3 million for the delivery and a hospital stay of only three days. Several hospitals in New York have specialized in deliveries for the Rich and Famous. The best is undoubtedly Mount Sinai, with its beautiful view of Central Park and the Manhattan skyline – this is where Gwyneth Paltrow and P. Diddy brought their children into the world. The hospital offers à la carte massages and afternoon tea and cookies. The exclusive Klingenstein Pavilion in Mount Sinai on Fifth Avenue has luxury suites with a variety of spa experience-oriented rooms. Only $4,000 a day!

1,776 FEET

I WTC

One World Trade Center is New York's tallest building. It is exactly 1,776 feet tall, symbolizing the year of the signing of the Declaration of Independence.

5.94 FEET

PATRICK

HIDDEN SPOTS
OF CENTRAL PARK

CENTRAL PARK

HIDDEN SPOTS OF CENTRAL PARK
CENTRAL PARK

🕐 2 TO 3 HOURS

1. CENTRAL PARK SIGHTSEEING BIKE RENTAL
2. WOLLMAN ICE SKATING RINK
3. CENTRAL PARK CAROUSEL
4. THE DAIRY VISITOR CENTER AND GIFT SHOP
5. OLMSTED FLOWER BED
6. SHAKESPEARE & COLUMBUS STATUE
7. BALTO STATUE
8. BETHESDA FOUNTAIN
9. HANS CHRISTIAN ANDERSEN STATUE
10. THE LOEB CENTRAL PARK BOATHOUSE
11. ALICE IN WONDERLAND STATUE
12. CLEOPATRA'S NEEDLE
13. THE METROPOLITAN MUSEUM OF ART
14. FRED LEBOW STATUE
15. SOLOMON R. GUGGENHEIM MUSEUM
16. JACQUELINE KENNEDY ONASSIS RESERVOIR
17. NORTH MEADOW SOFTBALL FIELD 9
18. LAMPPOST 102
19. CENTRAL PARK TENNIS CENTER
20. DELACORTE THEATER
21. SHAKESPEARE GARDEN
22. BELVEDERE CASTLE
23. STRAWBERRY FIELDS
24. SHEEP MEADOW
25. TAVERN ON THE GREEN
26. LE PAIN QUOTIDIEN
27. NEW YORK ATHLETIC CLUB
28. PETROSSIAN

New York's gigantic green lung is heavy stuff enough but the park still has more little gems in store. Ever heard of Strawberry Fields, Belvedere Castle, and the Shakespeare Garden? You could always go there for elaborate walks but the best way to discover all of Central Park's charming nooks is by bike! This allows you to catch a lot in a short time and easily reach the park's north, an area many tourists make the mistake of passing over.

❶ CENTRAL PARK SIGHTSEEING BIKE RENTAL

56th St., between 5th and 6th Ave.

www.centralparksightseeing.com

Brace yourself or race yourself. Got a helmet, lock, and bike basket? Before leaving, also make sure you inspect the brakes, tires, saddle, gears, and stand. All check? Then you're ready to go pedaling. Central park is close by, but be extremely careful on those 100 yards to the park!

❷ WOLLMAN ICE SKATING RINK

www.wollmanskatingrink.com

🕐 Mo.-Tu. 10 a.m.-2:30 a.m., We.-Th. 10 a.m.-10 p.m., Fr.-Sa. 10 a.m.-11 p.m., Su. 10 a.m.-9 p.m.

This ice skating rink is now called Trump Skating Rink because Donald is also an avid ice skater. From October to April you can show off your skills here or torment your tailbone.

❸ CENTRAL PARK CAROUSEL

In the middle of the park, at 64th St.

This is the fourth merry-go-round on this location (the previous versions came to a fiery end). This masterpiece from 1908 comes from Coney Island in Brooklyn. For $3 a ride, children big and small can try in vain to pass the other jockeys on one of the 57 horses. Giddy-up!

❹ THE DAIRY VISITOR CENTER AND GIFT SHOP

In the middle of the park, at 65th St.

In 1870, when dairy products were scarce, families with children came here to enjoy fresh milk and ice cream. Nowadays, this Victorian cottage serves as an information booth for visitors. The only milking takes place among the tourists in the souvenir shop.

❺ OLMSTED FLOWER BED

Aan Literary Walk, East 66th St.

This flowerbed was laid in honor of Frederik Law Olmsted's 150th birthday. He and Calvert Vaux were the architects of Central Park. The flowerbed lies at the start of The Mall, a walkway flanked by American elms and ending at Bethesda Terrace. The Mall is the only straight line in Central Park.

❻ SHAKESPEARE & COLUMBUS STATUE

On Literary Walk, East 66th St.

The Literary Walk, the first section of The Mall, features statues of renowned writers. The "odd man out" is Christopher Columbus. The discoverer of America (if for convenience's sake you briefly disregard the Vikings, Native Americans, and possibly the Chinese) certainly deserves an effigy. One minor hitch: Shakespeare's back was disrespectfully turned to Columbus. Since the pedestal was too heavy, only the statue was turned around, which explains why the plaque on Shakespeare's statue is on "the back."

❼ BALTO STATUE

Central Park East, at 67th St.
A national hero, this courageous husky from Alaska stands in honor of his expedition team. He guided them over ice and snow to their remote destination, where they were to deliver lifesaving medicines. In so doing, the Eskimo dog helped prevent children in the Far North from becoming victims of a diphtheria epidemic.

❽ BETHESDA FOUNTAIN

In the middle of the park, at 72nd St.
This beautiful statue is known as Angel of the Waters. It is the only statue from the original blueprints for Central Park and was designed by Emma Stebbins. She was the first female artist ever to be granted a public tender. The statue commemorates the construction of the Croton Aquaduct in 1842, which brought pure water to the city. Thanks to its

appearance in scores of movies and TV shows such as Home Alone, Gossip Girl, and Stuart Little, the fountain has itself become a genuine movie star. But please, no pictures.

❾ HANS CHRISTIAN ANDERSEN STATUE

Central Park East, at 74th St.
For his 150th birthday, the world famous writer of fairy tales was given a statue in Central Park next to the Conservatory Water. With thanks to the Danish-American community. The sculpture is meant to be climbed: Set an example and go for it.

❿ THE LOEB CENTRAL PARK BOATHOUSE

East 72nd St. and 5th Ave.
www.thecentralparkboathouse.com
🕐 Mo.-Fr. noon-3:45 p.m.,
Sa.-Su. 9:30 a.m.-4 p.m.
No idea how to use an oar? Perfect! Then you won't stick out among all the other tourists renting a boat here. Otherwise, it'll be 50% schadenfreude and 50% irritation. But as long as it's not too busy, it's quite fun. You can also get a bite to eat at the Boathouse but it's about as touristy as it gets. Expect killer views, mediocre food, bad service,

and a price to quality ratio that will make you want to tear your hair out. Wanna bet the tip's already been added to the bill?

⓫ ALICE IN WONDERLAND STATUE

Central Park East, at 75th St.
Feel free to take a seat on Alice's mushroom. This statue is also meant to be clambered on. The philanthropist George Delacorte had it made in honor of his wife Margarita and made a gift of it to all children. Good times for the offspring, good pictures for the parents.

⓬ CLEOPATRA'S NEEDLE

Central Park East, at 81st St.
This Ancient Egyptian obelisk is a sibling of the one in London. This massive sculpture weighs more than 220 tons and, at a respectable age of 3,500 years, it is the oldest in Central Park by a long shot. It took 32 horses, a whole lot more manpower, and a couple of months to transfer this colossus from the Hudson to its current location. The obelisk comfortably withstood the test of time until the pollution of recent decades made extensive restoration inevitable.

⑬ THE METROPOLITAN MUSEUM OF ART

1000 5th Ave. and 82nd St.
www.metmuseum.org
🕐 Su.-Th. 10 a.m.-5:30 p.m., Fr. and Sa. 10 a.m.-9 p.m.

With 2 million objects, the art collection is the largest in the US. Unless you have a month's vacation, choices have to be made. If you've shuffled yourself to exhaustion, you can take a break on the roof and enjoy a drink with a view of Central Park. The best news? The entrance fee is only a suggestion. How much you pay is up to you.

⑭ FRED LEBOW STATUE

Central Park East, at 90th St.
Fred Lebow organized the first New York City Marathon, which originally took place exclusively within Central Park. The first edition had 127 participants; today there are no fewer than 50,000. The statue is a popular meeting point for runners. When the Marathon's taking place, it's transferred to the finish line so Fred can personally greet the winners.

⑮ SOLOMON R. GUGGENHEIM MUSEUM

1071 5th Ave., between 88th and 89th St.
www.guggenheim.org
🕐 Su.-We. and Fr. 10 a.m.-5:45 p.m. (closed Th.), Sa. 10a.m.-7:45 p.m.

Frank Lloyd Wright, the Guggenheim's architect, once said that his design would reduce the Metropolitan Museum to a protestant shed. Perhaps a bit over the top, but the building, inspired by a Babylonian pyramid, has certainly gained a respectable status in the world of art.

⑯ JACQUELINE KENNEDY ONASSIS RESERVOIR

Central Park, between 86th and 97th St.
This reservoir once supplied water to all of New York but, nowadays, its 135 million cubic feet of H2O would be depleted within four hours! Its moniker is a tribute to Jacqueline Kennedy, who lived with John Jr. and Caroline on Fifth Avenue and liked to come here for a jog.

⑰ NORTH MEADOW SOFTBALL FIELD 9

Central Park East, at 101st St.
The north side of Central Park is much less touristy. One clue to this is the abundance of sports fields teeming with New Yorkers. The Wall Street Journal once counted all the different sports practiced in the park. The result was 29, not counting squirrel hunting.

⑱ 18 KEEP YOUR EYES OPEN FOR LAMPPOST 102

Turn left at lamppost 102! Unless you've got a good pair of legs and have ambitions of conquering the peak of the Great Hill. In which case, you can now go straight on to the last bit of the park. Brave as a (mountain) lion!

⑲ CENTRAL PARK TENNIS CENTER

Central Park West, at 96th St.
www.centralparktenniscenter.com
🕐 Mo.-Su. 6:30 a.m.-8 p.m.

Land in Manhattan is expensive, resulting in a scarcity of sports grounds. Not so in Central Park, where there are no fewer than 30 courts. Also suitable for a bathroom break or for a quick snack.

⑳ DELACORTE THEATER

81 Central Park West, middle of the park, at 80th St.
🕐 Mo.-Su. 10 a.m.-7 p.m.

To queue or not to queue, that is the question. And the answer is an unqualified

"Yes!" This open-air theater in Central Park offers free Shakespeare every summer. All you need to do is show up on time to make sure you get tickets. If you're lucky, you'll get to see stars such as Meryl Streep and Al Pacino in action.

㉑ SHAKESPEARE GARDEN

Middle of the park, at 79th St.
⏲ Mo.-Su. 10 a.m.-5 p.m.

Since we're already on the subject of the Bard... Before you reach Belvedere Castle, you pass through Shakespeare Garden. No plays here, just a collection of all the flowers and plants hailed by Shakespeare in his works. Since he never mentioned dandelions, stinkhorns or cacti, it turned out beautifully.

㉒ BELVEDERE CASTLE

Middle of the park, at 79th St.

Time for a visit to Central Park's highest point. As the name suggests, one with a view. This was the only function ever fulfilled by this picturesque castle dating from 1865. The only wars fought here are over the best photo spots. Look out for Gargamel! Since the 2011 movie, he's been scheming to capture Smurfs here.

㉓ STRAWBERRY FIELDS

Central Park West, from 71st to 74th St.

If you think you'll really find strawberries here, you're in for a surprise. This monument to John Lennon takes its name from the Beatles song "Strawberry Fields Forever." His widow, Yoko Ono, still lives in the Dakota Building across the road, where Lennon was shot outside his front door. The memorial has become a place of reflection where 9/11 and other tragedies are commemorated.

㉔ SHEEP MEADOW

Central Park West, from 66th St. to 69th St.

The sheep that used to graze here were moved to safer havens during the Great Depression for fear they would be abducted by the starving. Nowadays it's a great place to lie in the sun, picnic, play Frisbee, etc., with a unique combination of natural and architectural beauty as a backdrop.

㉕ TAVERN ON THE GREEN

Central Park West & 67th St.
www.tavernonthegreen.com
⏲ Mo.-Fr. 11 a.m.-1 a.m.,
Sa.-Su. 9 a.m.-1 a.m.

Dining out in the world's chicest sheep pen. When the original occupants vacated the premises, the pen was converted into the famous Tavern on the Green. During times of financial straits, the house was closed for long periods but it's now open again for delicious dining. And, yes, there are also lamb chops on the menu.

㉖ LE PAIN QUOTIDIEN

Middle of the park, at 69th St.
www.lepainquotidien.com/us
⏲ Mo.-Su. 7 a.m.-4 p.m.

This Belgian concept has caught on. Now, there are more Pain Quotidiens in New York than in Belgium. Expect long lines on busy days – for the food as well as for the restrooms.

㉗ NEW YORK ATHLETIC CLUB

180 Central Park South
www.nyac.org
⏲ Always open.

Very few sports clubs can equal the NYAC's Olympic record. Among its members are scores of medalists from all the sports disciplines. The club's social and athletic center is its 24-story building, housing sports and relaxation equipment. But the club also has a blot on its record: For a long time it refused entry to Jews and blacks. Fortunately we are now in the 21st century.

ⓩ PETROSSIAN

182 W 58th St. betweem 5th and
6th Ave.

www.petrossian.com

🕑 Su.-Th. 11:30 a.m.-3 p.m. and 5 p.m.-
11 p.m., Fr.-Sa. 11:30 a.m.-3 and
5:30 p.m.-11 p.m.

Now that you're out of
the park, you better keep
your eyes on the road. But
the terracotta facade of
this unique and protect-
ed French Renaissance
style structure is virtually
impossible to ignore. Inside
is the Russian Petrossian
Restaurant, which with
caviar, foie gras and smoked
fish, guarantees a top-quali-
ty dinner. Enjoy your meal!
(But return your bike first.)

Arul

AN EMPIRE OF POOP

SANAVITA
508 East
12th St.,
between
Ave. A & B.
sanavita.org

The warmhearted and charming Arul is the mother of Seven Lightening and Naturale Dominique. She runs a holistic purification clinic, practices yoga and Pilates, and goes to a weekly pole-dancing class. She built her business, SanaVita, from scratch and specializes in *colon cleansing*. In her own words: she built an empire on poop. An empire with, by now, thirty employees.

Arul and I supported each other when we were just beginning. She deserves much respect for what she has achieved. Starting a business as a single mother is anything but simple. Especially if your company is all about feces. It didn't help her get an abundance of second dates either.

But times have changed. "People are dying to talk about poo," she says. All her clients want to watch the transparent section of her machine, the one where you see the waste whizz by. Typical for New Yorkers, Arul knows. They want to see what their dollars are buying. An intestinal sanitization as well as a show. I have to admit that this show is on my proverbial bucket list. In other words, I haven't had the, um, guts to let Arul cleanse my colon. For those who do plan to do it: Let me know how it went. Maybe I'll still take the plunge.

Arul is enamored with New York. She loves the city and its inhabitants. And although you may often hear that it isn't easy here for families with children, she can't imagine a better place to raise her son and daughter. If you ask her why, she waxes lyrical and talks about a friendly, open, and tolerant community where people help each other in an environment that offers an abundance of opportunities. The only thing you need is the courage to grasp them.

And she has that courage. Her last boyfriend was someone she met in the subway. She approached him and asked if he wanted to go to a movie. That was the beginning of a relationship that lasted three years. It's obvious that Arul's attitude hasn't bogged her down.

A Tip
from Arul

MR. SUNDAY
Varying locations
www.mistersaturdaynight.com
Mr. Sunday is an open-air
Sunday party held in Brooklyn during the summer
months. It starts early in the
evening, the atmosphere
is open and informal, and
all ages are welcome. Even
your faithful four-footed
friend can come, that is, if
he or she likes house music.
Respect and fun for everyone are the basic ingredients of this estival event.

Zen York

New York City conjures up images of busy-ness, stress, and a fast-paced life. Anyone who denies this has probably never been to New York. Even so, the city has much to offer for anyone seeking peace and wanting to live healthily. Take the countless parks, galleries, cultural centers, and museums, as well as the profusion of massage parlors, spas, and wellness centers. Also tai chi, yoga, and meditation are immensely popular here. And food-wise there's a full choice of gluten-free, vegetarian, and vegan restaurants. If it gets too hectic for you in Manhattan, then maybe it's time for a short visit to one of the other boroughs. The options are too many to mention: The botanical garden and zoo in the Bronx, Prospect Park in Brooklyn and Astoria Park in Queens are just a few of the places where you could normalize your stress levels. The ultimate relaxing element is the water. It's everywhere. All over New York you can stroll and bike along it, fish, watch a movie, party, eat, date, and much more. The epitome of relaxation is a sailing boat tour among all the islands and famous bridges. After you embark from the harbor, you briefly leave the clamor of the city behind and can enjoy the quiet, the nature, and the sublime panoramas.

MANHATTAN YACHT CLUB
North Cove Marina, 385 South End Ave.
www.myc.org
This marina lies near Battery Park and the old World Financial Center/ new World Trade Center. The Arabella yacht serves as a nightclub for all New York's sailing enthusiasts. It's south of the yacht basin, but open only to club members and guests.

New Patrick

RENEW DAY SPA
42 Bowery, Chinatown
www.renewdayspa.net
Give your tired feet some well-deserved attention from time to time. They deserve it after slogging around town all day. I regularly visit the Renew Day Spa. Don't expect a luxurious entourage (far from it, in fact), but they do give the best foot and full body massages in New York City at the extremely modest prices of $22 and $36 respectively, you walk out the door an hour later feeling reborn.

Olivia

MY BODY MY TEMPLE

My becoming an American citizen was a pretty stressful occasion. Wife and daughter couldn't attend; the TV production team was waiting outside in the rain and was denied entry. But what really got me that day was that my suit, which I hadn't worn in years, didn't fit anymore: I couldn't get my pants button fastened. The verdict was there on the scales for all to see: 231 pounds. Something had to be done about that. My sweet wife gifted me with a fitness club membership and my good friend Robert advised me to pay a visit to Olivia, fitness model and boxing coach.

The stereotypical figure of the stout American is hard to find in New York. And when you finally do come across a heavyset person you can just about be sure it's a tourist. New Yorkers are health freaks. Everyone is following some purification treatment and just about everybody has a gym membership. You don't become a fitness coach here just like that. Long Islander Olivia underwent a three-month training course and had to pass four strict "auditions" before being accepted as an indoor cycling coach. Fortunately, she already possessed a sharp tongue. She began her career among the fierce Wall Street businessmen. But the bronzed all-American athlete quickly realized she wasn't made for an office job. After three years, she made the switch to the world of professional sports.

Olivia is not only an indoor cycling coach and fitness model, but also a boxing coach. Not only to be able to deal with precarious situations – New York has never been safer, though you never know – but because of the sport's beauty. You need to be skilled and in great shape, and you need a steady mental cool-headedness to help you deal more effectively with the demands of a bustling city. She gives classes in her "boxing boutique" – the same as a boxing club but with nicer showers and more cozy seats – to students, young mothers, and men coming straight from the office. I'm strongly seriously signing up so I can train my right hook and do something about my girth. Want to know how that's going? Join a tour!

A Tip
from Patrick

FREEMANS RESTAURANT IN FREEMAN ALLEY

On the Lower East Side there's a little alley hiding between Bowery and Chrystie Street. Freeman Alley is a side street off Rivington that culminates in the hipster-haunted Freemans Restaurant. Awaiting you inside is a pastoral interior adorned with stuffed animal heads; a room that closely resembles a hunting cabin. The food has elicited many a hallelujah and the brunch is a must. You have to try the artichoke dip.

A Tip from Patrick

ILLEGAL INK

"My body is my temple," is the motto of hordes of health-obsessed New Yorkers. Many of them don't flinch from digging deep into their pockets to provide that temple with various decorations. That's right, I'm talking about tattoos. Believe it or not, until 1997 tattooing was prohibited in New York. This restriction followed a hepatitis B epidemic in the 1960s, which the authorities pounced on in order to ban tattoos and a whole bunch of other stuff on the grounds of bad hygiene. Tattoo buffs challenged the decision but were told by the court that "only unnatural and deviant persons would indulge in such barbaric practices" and that, obviously, no exceptions could be made. But after this crazy law was repealed in 1997, masses of tattoo parlors popped up all over the city.

Tattoo parlors in New York

EAST SIDE INK

97 Ave. B between 6th and 7th St.
www.eastsideinktattoo.com
This parlor already existed before tattooing was officially permitted. They do excellent work here including laser removals for those having second thoughts. Rihanna has become part of the furniture here, although she once got the owners into trouble after wielding a needle herself and posting the pictures on the internet. The police rewarded her endeavors with a penalty: Tattooing without a license is a misdemeanor and carries a $2,000 fine. After hearing that, Rihanna was undoubtedly on the verge of despair.

NEW YORK ADORNED

47 2nd Ave., between 2nd and 3rd St.
www.nyadorned.com
At New York Adorned they're professional and experienced. With a beautiful interior to boot. And why not, considering their services cost between $150 and $200 an hour. Plus sales tax, of course. But that's got to be better than waking up with a spelling mistake or 53 stars on your face...

GET THERE ON TIME
A renowned tattoo parlor usually has a long waiting list. So make an appointment well in advance.

I bui

an en

on po

t
mpire
oop.

ARUL

Robert

PICTURE PERFECT PARK

My search for the right photographer for this book brought me to Robert, a good friend of Allison's. Being able to snag him for this project makes me very proud. Because this New Yorker from the Upper West Side is not just any old photographer.

As a photographer for the New York Times, every day he made portraits of the world's greatest. Not just anyone is visited by Alec Baldwin for a series of portrait photos, or gets the chance to stand next to Alicia Keys and Jay-Z in the sold-out stadium for the World Series. For Justin Bieber's book project, he even travelled around the world for several months with the teen idol. Never without his earplugs of course. And at the Hurricane Sandy benefit concert, for a whole day, he rubbed shoulders with Kanye West, The Rolling Stones, Paul McCartney, Billy Joel, and Bon Jovi. The list goes on.

In addition, Robert is one fantastic source of information for a tour guide. His work takes him to places mere mortals can only dream of. And although these places are not necessarily open to the public, they do always provide interesting background information.

Robert is in love with Central Park. He unhesitatingly takes on any commission in any way related to it. He showed me some breathtaking spots such as the bewitching path bursting with cherry blossom on the southwest side of the reservoir. And the equally enchanting northeast point of The Lake where he married his girlfriend. The farther north you go in the park, the fewer tourists and the more locals you'll encounter. With a bit of luck you may even find areas where you can stroll alone.

A few Tips from Robert

CHERRY BLOSSOM BRIDLE PATH

Of the estimated 500 Somei Yoshino cherry blossoms in Central Park, many are situated on the west side, at 90th Street and the Bridle Path.

ORIENTATION IN CENTRAL PARK

A good way to find your way in the park is to use the lampposts. Most lampposts have a number at their base. The first two digits refer to the nearest street outside the park. For example, if the number is 7902, you know you're nearest to 79th Street. So you can always be sure of your location.

RIVERSIDE PARK

When you're in the Upper West Side area, be sure to visit the Riverside Park on Manhattan's west bank, where you can enjoy a leisurely promenade or bike ride, all the while reveling in the wonderful view of the Hudson. You really get the feeling that you're on an island here.

A few Tips from Patrick

THANKSGIVING DAY PARADE BALLOON INFLATION
77th St. and Central Park West
social.macys.com/parade

The Thanksgiving Day Parade is a world-famous event that draws 3.5 million spectators every year and is viewed at home by many more. On the preceding day, you can watch the giant balloons being inflated in preparation for the parade. This in itself is an attraction and a good alternative if you prefer to avoid the commotion.

RACCOONS IN CENTRAL PARK

They look really cute, but beware! The estimated 300 raccoons nesting in Central Park have sharp claws and teeth and can behave very aggressively. Fortunately, it isn't a common occurrence, but there are recorded incidents of passers-by having to contend with rather unfriendly raccoons. Moreover, tests have shown that a considerable number of the animals are carriers of rabies and other unpleasant diseases. But the bold creatures are undaunted by humans. So keep a safe distance!

TAVERN ON THE GREEN
67th St. and Central Park West
www.tavernonthegreen.com

Following four years of absence due to financial straits, one of America's most renowned restaurants is back. Tavern on the Green rejected a bid from Donald Trump, underwent a radical facelift, and now has room for 700 diners. There isn't much left of the original interior and the menu has also been overhauled. Considering the location, the prices are reasonable. A main course costs between $25 and $55 and most dishes are under $30. Not including tax and tips, but including a fantastic park.

Central Park in Figures

Central Park is one of the world's largest constructed parks and New York City's green lung. The park runs from 5th Avenue to 8th Avenue and from 59th Street to 110th Street, which makes it half a mile wide and 2.5 miles long. Without this green oasis, New York would be virtually unlivable. Parks account for 14% of New York's total area. Central Park's share is 6%. The term "park" is actually a discredit to this constructed marvel. The most frequented park in the United States is more or less its own city. At every hour of the day there is something to be experienced; from chess tournaments and dog shows to free massages. An absolute must-see (and do) for every tourist *and* for every New Yorker.

CENTRAL PARK

20,000 TREES

40 MILLION VISITORS

60 MILES OF WALKING PATHS

9,000 BENCHES

1,400 ZOO WITH ANIMALS

58 MILLION ANNUAL BUDGET

1000s OF SQUIR-RELS

30 TENNIS COURTS

26 BASEBALL FIELDS

300 RACCOONS

200 BIRD SPECIES

12 HAND-BALL COURTS

1
CASTLE
AUDITORIUM
MUSEUM
PUPPET THEATER
GALLERY
MERRY-GO-ROUND
WEATHER STATION
POLICE STATION

36 BRIDGES

2
BASKETBALL COURTS
RESTAURANTS
ICE SKATING RINKS

FEATURED IN OVER

240 MOVIES

21 PLAY-GROUNDS

AREA
843 ACRES

OPENED IN

1857

7 LAKES

HOLY HARLEM

HARLEM

HOLY HARLEM
HARLEM

🕐 3 TO 4 HOURS

1. SUBWAY STOP B, C
2. HUNGARIAN PASTRY SHOP
3. THE CATHEDRAL CHURCH OF ST. JOHN THE DIVINE
4. TOM'S RESTAURANT
5. COLUMBIA UNIVERSITY
6. RIVERSIDE CHURCH
7. GENERAL GRANT NATIONAL MEMORIAL
8. AMC MAGIC JOHNSON HARLEM 9
9. APOLLO THEATER
10. HOTEL THERESA
11. THE STUDIO MUSEUM IN HARLEM
12. BARAWINE
13. CLINTON'S OFFICE
14. RED ROOSTER
15. ASTOR ROW HOUSES
16. HARLEM YMCA
17. SCHOMBURG CENTER FOR RESEARCH IN BLACK CULTURE
18. ABYSSINIAN BAPTIST CHURCH
19. STRIVERS' ROW

Are you ready for an exploration of this mind-blowing neighborhood in the north of Manhattan? Your route includes inspiring gospel services, heavenly soul food, stunning art and culture, along with breath-taking architecture. Whether it's music, human rights, religion, or gastronomy: Harlem has made its mark on all aspects of society. Not only in New York, but also throughout the United States and far beyond. This path takes you through everything that makes Harlem so unique. It is justifiably hallowed ground for the black community and of inestimable value for cultural world heritage. You're really going to dig Holy Harlem.

❶ SUBWAY STOP B, C
110th and Central Park West
Your pilgrimage begins appropriately at this steep hill. Turn your back to Central Park for the moment and go west. Go climb a mountain!

❷ HUNGARIAN PASTRY SHOP
1030 Amsterdam Ave., between 110th and 111th St.
🕐 Mo.-Fr. 8 a.m.-11:30 p.m., Sa.-Su. 8:30 a.m.-11:30 p.m.
If, after this precipitous climb, you haven't yet bitten the dust, there will be other things to sink your teeth into. Before moving on to the sacramental bread, why not start with a breakfast of delicious coffee and cookies at this Hungarian bakery? Or you could do the cathedral first.

❸ THE CATHEDRAL CHURCH OF ST. JOHN THE DIVINE
1047 Amsterdam Ave., between 110th and 113th St.
www.stjohndivine.org
🕐 Mo.-Su. 7:30 a.m.-6 p.m.
St. John will have to keep his shirt on because this edifice is far from finished. Of course, we're talking here about the construction of one of the world's largest cathedrals. Two world wars and a fire haven't exactly sped things up but, nevertheless, after 20 years of construction, this masterpiece is impressive enough. Allow yourself the time to enjoy the stained glass windows. If you look closely, you'll discover not only biblical scenes but also modern ones: The sinking Titanic, car races, and a TV prototype are all depicted.

❹ TOM'S RESTAURANT
2880 Broadway
www.tomsrestaurant.net
🕐 Su.-We. 6 a.m.-1:30 a.m., Th.-Sa. 24/24
This diner is the salvation of any Columbia University student with nocturnal cravings. It inspired Suzanne Vega's hit, "Tom's Diner" (you'll definitely recognize it if you hear it) and also regularly satisfied Jerry Seinfeld's culinary needs. The building is actually owned by Columbia University. Barnard College, Columbia's art academy, is around the corner. Tu tu tu du, tu tu du du...

❺ COLUMBIA UNIVERSITY
116th and Broadway
www.columbia.edu
This is the campus where the greatest minds are groomed for stardom. No fewer than 43 Nobel Prize winners and 29 heads of state (including Barack Obama) graduated from this prestigious Ivy League university. Before you rush to the enrollment office, hoping to rule a country one day: annual tuition is $45,000.

❻ RIVERSIDE CHURCH
490 Riverside Drive and 122nd St.
www.theriversidechurchny.org
🕐 Mo.-Su. 7 a.m.-10 p.m.
John Rockefeller (you know, that rich guy) is the cornerstone of this stunning, awe-inspiring church.

Figuratively, of course. This makes him the proud owner of the heaviest carillon on earth, which chimes 392 feet above street level in honor of his mother. The parish is also doing okay. It has an annual budget of $14 million and employs more than 120 people.

⑦ GENERAL GRANT NATIONAL MEMORIAL

Riverside Drive and 123rd St
www.nps.gov
⏰ We.-Mo. 9 a.m.-5 p.m.

Mister Ulysses S. Grant, Commanding General of the Army and 18th President of the United States, wasn't too crazy about racist cone-heads (with or without pointy hoods). He won the Civil War, defeated the Ku Klux Klan, and fought for African-American civil rights. This well-deserved shack was his reward. "Let us have peace," he once said when he was nominated for President.

⑧ AMC MAGIC JOHNSON HARLEM 9

2309 Frederick Douglass Blvd., corner of 124th St.
www.amctheatres.com

Mr. Johnson sought further success after quitting basketball and, sure enough, he became a businessman. He pulled a small empire out of his hat, including Best Buy, the T.G.I. Friday's restaurant chain, a real estate company with a ten-digit value, and Magic Johnson Theaters. Although he's sold the latter, it still bears his name. If you want to grab a movie, you have to go here. With emphasis on "have to": It's the only cinema in Harlem.

⑨ APOLLO THEATER

253 West 125th Street, between A .C. Powell Jr. Blvd. and Frederick Douglass Blvd.
www.apollotheater.org
www.amateurnight.org

Grab the mike and your chance for stardom during Amateur Night at the Apollo Theater. Major stars, such as James Brown, Stevie Wonder, and Michael Jackson have already set the example. Are you more talented at cheering or booing? Then you're desperately needed in the audience.

⑩ HOTEL THERESA

2082 A .C. Powell Jr. Blvd, between W 124th and 125th St.
www.nps.gov

This hotel used to be known as "The Waldorf of Harlem" and in its heyday was as magnificent as it was indispensable: Hotels in Midtown Manhattan would not admit non-whites. This made Hotel Theresa *the* location for the Afro-American high society. The presence of numerous well-known artists, politicians, and athletes drew the crowds. It was also teeming when Fidel Castro and John F. Kennedy stayed there. But people got smart and racism was sent packing. This caused occupancy to dwindle and the hotel to stop functioning as such. In the early 1970s, the 300 rooms were born again as offices.

⑪ THE STUDIO MUSEUM IN HARLEM

144 W 125th St.
www.studiomuseum.org
⏰ Th.-Fr. 12 noon-9 p.m., Sa. 10 a.m.-6 p.m., Su. 12 noon-6 p.m.

This museum is dedicated to Afro-American art because "black truly is beautiful." The collection is mostly 19th and 20th century but contemporary artists are also given a chance. Often enough, Harlem itself is the subject of the exhibitions. The museum is more of a gallery due to its modest size. Deejays tempt you to dance among the paintings on Friday nights and on Sundays admission is free!

⑫ BARAWINE

310 Lenox Ave., between 125th and
126th St.
www.barawine.com
🕐 Mo.-We. 4 p.m.-10 p.m.,
Th.-Fr. 4 p.m.-11 p.m., Sa. 11:30 a.m.-
11 p.m., Su. 11:30 a.m.-10 p.m.
Classy brunch and dinner
in a European decor. Its
all-you-can-drink mimo-
sas help make it easily
recognizable: White folk
teetering and tottering as
they leave.

⑬ CLINTON'S OFFICE

55 W 125th St., between 5th and
Lenox Ave.
To show support for the
neighborhood, the former
President moved his office
to the center of Harlem.
This promptly led to a new
string of lingerie and cigar
stores in the area. It was
also good news for taxpay-
ers because Bill's rent here
is much lower. A great example to which many can't
hold a candle (or cigar).

⑭ RED ROOSTER

310 Lenox Ave., between 125th and
126th St.
www.redroosterharlem.com
🕐 Mo.-Su. 11:30 a.m.-3 p.m.,
17:30 p.m.-10:30 p.m.
Red Rooster serves up better soul food with a modern
twist to keep up with the
constantly demographically
diversifying neighborhood.

Non-edible culture is served
here too. There is often live
music and the art on display
is carefully selected in con-
sultation with the Studio
Museum.

⑮ ASTOR ROW HOUSES

W 130th St., between 5th and
Lenox Ave.
A front *and* a back yard
in Manhattan? Not many
Manhattanites have such
luck. But the residents
of the 28 townhouses on
Astor Row do. The facades
and Victorian verandas
from the late 1800s were
renovated, a century later,
at the instigation of Brooke
Astor, the wife of the great-
great-grandson of John
Jacob Astor, better known
as the first multimillionaire
in American history.

⑯ HARLEM YMCA

180 W 135th St., between Lenox Ave.
and A.C. Powell Jr. Blvd.
www.ymcanyc.org
It's still fun to stay at the
YMCA (even if you're not a
Native American or a con-
struction worker). This pro-
tected monument was and
still is an important cultural
and recreation center for
the black community. "The
Y" has a gym, a basketball
court, a swimming pool, and
more than 200 rooms. Im-
portant personalities, such

as Malcolm X and Martin
Luther King, were regular
guests.

⑰ SCHOMBURG CENTER FOR RESEARCH IN BLACK CULTURE

515 Malcolm X Blvd., between 135th
and 136th St.
www.nypl.org/locations/schomburg
🕐 Mo. 10 a.m.-6 p.m., Tu.-Th. 12 noon-
8 p.m., Fr. 10 a.m.-6 p.m., Su. closed
This center is the New York
Public Library's research
department and archives
for all things related to African culture and diaspora.
Arturo Schomburg was
an important figure in the
Harlem Renaissance and an
advocate of rights for and
recognition of Afro-Latin
Americans and Afro-Ameri-
cans. Thanks to him, there's
a treasure trove of information to be unearthed here.

⑱ ABYSSINIAN BAPTIST CHURCH

132 W 138th Street, between
A. C. Powell Jr. Blvd. and Lenox Ave.
www.abyssinian.org
🕐 Su. 11 a.m.
The Abyssinian Church
eagerly praises the
Almighty on Sundays.
If you want a bit of the
action you'll have to get up
early. The service draws a
lot of tourists, with lines
starting as early as 9 a.m.
There is no entry fee but
donations are expected.

Dress modestly, don't take pictures, and show respect or you'll have to leave before the gospel.

⑲ STRIVERS' ROW

W 138th and W 139th St. and A.C. Powell Jr. and F. Douglass Blvd.
The 19th century row houses on Strivers' Row are historical gems of great architectural value. Strivers' Row was originally intended for the more affluent white middle class but times dictated otherwise. White or black, anyone who could snag a dwelling here had it made. Strictly for go-getters, which explains the name.

MILDRED AND JOYCE

NEW YORK MOMS

Meet two charming sisters, pedigree New Yorkers, who were loyal customers of Petite Abeille, the Belgian restaurant where I used to work. I would always greet them the traditional Belgian way, with a big kiss on the cheek. They were so charmed by this that, over time, I evolved from host to adopted son.

Ever since, they have followed my life from a distance. If I didn't call every day, it would mean trouble. One day they'd go to Belgium, they said. Being eager to learn, they wanted to discover everything. They also looked everything up. This led to their discovery, and great amusement, that I come from a country so small that its own name doesn't fit within the country on the map. Our adventures as a close trio, however,

ended abruptly in March of 2016 when, to my great sorrow, Joyce passed away. On the next page you'll find an elaborate homage to one of the loveliest people I ever met in the city of dreams.

The sisters' life story is admirable. Mildred was a doctor, Joyce a lawyer, and all this at a time when this was anything but ordinary for a woman, especially an African American woman. Thanks to them, I learned about the culture and history of Harlem, where the black community is deeply rooted. They took me to bona fide gospel services where the churchgoers sing – and dance – with all their strength. But it didn't end there. They also took me in tow to Broadway shows and operas. They were determined to spoil me as the "son they never had" and when my Marie was born they were overjoyed.

IN MEMORIAM JOYCE (SEPTEMBER 10 1923 – MARCH 21 2016)

She felt too young to be called "Grandma." I had to make do with "Aunt." A few days before my 40th birthday, Joyce, our loving oasis of tranquility in New York, passed away. Joyce, who always took the time to welcome us and whose door always stood wide open. For her unlimited tact and her respect for others, she will always serve as a model to us. "When they go low, we go high," Michelle Obama said at the Democratic Convention in 2016. There is no motto more fitting to Joyce's life. No matter how hard life was, growing up as an African American, no matter how she was treated, she would always react the same way: with dignity. We will continue to miss her for a long time.

A FEW TIPS FROM MILDRED

An authentic gospel service in Harlem is one thing you've just got to experience. The hundreds of churches in Harlem often stand in stark contrast to the magnificence and splendor of edifices such as Trinity Church, but at no cost to the fervor of faith. On the contrary.

ABYSSINIAN BAPTIST CHURCH

132 Odell Clark Pl., 138th St., between Adam Clayton Powell Jr. and Lenox Ave.
www.abyssinian.org
This church has enjoyable gospel services but has become quite touristy.

SAINT MATTHEW'S BAPTIST CHURCH

43 Macombs Pl, West 151st St.
www.smbcharlem.org
St. Matthew's is a little way up in Harlem and is a lot less touristy. Lisa Jenkins is the first female pastor to lead the church in its 90 years in existence. The parish is particularly active and does much for the community. One of her many initiatives is helping the mom-and-pop stores in their battle with the big conglomerates that are slowly but surely taking over everywhere, including Harlem.

FUN FACT

Once a month weapons can be turned in at St. Matthew's in exchange for food or clothing coupons. This collaborative project with the NYPD for making the neighborhood safer has borne fruit. The church is also a great source of support for teenage mothers and HIV patients.

HARLEM

When I sound out my clients' knowledge of New York's districts, "Harlem" is invariably one of the answers. Harlem certainly isn't the most well-known or the most frequented part of New York, but one way or another, everyone has heard of it. And with good reason. As the cradle of the Harlem Renaissance, the neighborhood was a cornerstone of the history and culture of the black American community. This movement in the 1920s and 30s brought forth an incredible gathering of artists, singers, dancers, writers, politicians, and intellectuals and became a source of inspiration to succeeding generations. Religion always plays an important role in this community. This is evidenced by the presence of more than four hundred houses of prayer in Harlem, some of which are absolute gems. And if you've ever wanted to experience a gospel service, there's no better place for it than Harlem. Harlem is also the destination of choice for delicious soul food and Southern cuisine, which originated during the years of slavery. If you visit the neighborhood, be sure to stop at the Apollo Theater. Countless big names from the entertainment industry started their careers here, such as The Jackson Five, James Brown, Stevie Wonder, Ella Fitzgerald, and Aretha Franklin, to name but a few.

FUN FACT

The Harlem shake is an actual dance, based on the Ethiopian dance Eskista. Just to be absolutely clear: It has nothing to do with the internet meme from 2013, a video in which a group of people go wild to the sounds of a sample of the song "Harlem Shake."

FUN FACT

The Apollo Theater was originally a burlesque club open only to white audiences. Later, in 1934, it became the first theater to open its doors to a mixed public. For years now, on Wednesdays, it features the famous Amateur Night. If you're thinking of signing up, keep in mind that past winners include Ella Fitzgerald and Jimmy Hendrix.

RED ROOSTER

310 Lenox Ave., between 125th and 126st St.
www.redroosterharlem.com
Hungry from all those hallelujahs, amens, and singing? There's a tasty brunch waiting for you at the Red Rooster. Live music and traditional comfort food are served here, in the tradition of American Southern cuisine. This is mesmeric Harlem at its best.

SYLVIA'S

328 Malcolm X Boulevard
www.sylviasrestaurant.com
This restaurant may be very well known but it's annoyingly touristy and the quality of the food leaves much to be desired. The prices aren't bad but there are better places for a first-time soul food experience.

APOLLO THEATER

253 West 125th St.
www.amateurnight.org

IT TA

A SPE

PERSO

LIVE H

KES
CIAL
ON TO
IERE.

DANIEL

DANIEL

AND THE OSCAR GOES TO... BABY TWINS

Daniel came to New York years ago to become an actor. Fat chance. He went through the customary route of badly paid jobs and auditions until the Gray Line, the well-known touring bus company where I also worked for a while, hired him as a guide. Being a history major, the job was right up his alley and he decided to turn it into a career. Not much later he became a member, and even chairman, of GANYC (Guide Association of New York City). That's where I met him.

Both being city guides, we naturally liked to exchange information about our mutual passion. There's always something new to be discovered. We also like to share stories about our guided tour experiences. Such as moving a group of tourists to the next subway car because someone decided to relieve himself among the tightly-packed commuters during rush hour. Or hurrying to the rescue of dignified Bible Belt ladies who had been invited to touch the bare and sweaty *moobs* of a voluptuous passer-by.

But these are just anecdotes. It's important to Daniel to give people the right impression of New York. There is no shortage of unwarranted prejudice against the city. That everyone there is impolite and arrogant, for example. But no one leaves New York still hanging on to these misconceptions. Unless we're dealing with MTA (Metropolitan Transportation Authority) personnel, he adds laughingly. Another classic is that it's too hectic to live there, generally uttered by those who haven't gotten further than the touristy section of Manhattan. People also always want to know whether you really can kill someone by throwing a penny off the Empire State Building. And whether there really are alligators living in the sewers. Not. Initially, New York brings many newcomers to their knees. An initiation rite to which many fellow city dwellers, including yours truly, can testify. It was no different with Daniel. The woman who put a roof over his head when he became homeless died in his arms. Not much later he also lost his job. Nevertheless, he sees these experiences as a good thing. He's learned to stand up and fight for himself. And New York has other sides. Sympathy and solidarity can be seen and felt, more than anywhere else. For instance, when a total stranger offers you a room, or the time when, in the subway, a lady went over and sat next to Daniel and silently handed him her handkerchief when the tears were rolling down his cheeks. All this forged an everlasting bond between him and this unique city, defining him as a true New Yorker.

How would Daniel characterize a New Yorker? Independent, persevering, fearless, and possessing a big heart and even bigger dreams. If you can make it here, you can make it anywhere. And you can never start too soon. Daniel's twins, though still in diapers, are already making it in Hollywood. The apples of his eye, Liliana and Evangeline, share the role of a baby in the Netflix production *Tallulah*. And as if all this isn't incredible enough to you, hold on to your hats: The twins were the New York Times' favorites for the Oscar for best actress.

A FEW TIPS FROM DANIEL

IN ADVANCE
Book your guide in plenty of time. He can prepare for your arrival and makes things easier for you during your visit. He can assist you in planning your schedule and help you with subway tickets, tickets for cruises, Broadway shows, attractions, restaurant reservations, limousines, helicopters, etc.

WHEN YOU'RE HERE
"Don't be a touron!" This is the term for the typical dumb tourist (a tourist and a moron). Be aware of the customs and standards and respect them. The locals will appreciate it and it will only be to your advantage.

BILL'S BAR & BURGER
Rockefeller Center, 16 West 51st St. on 5th Ave.
Bill's Meatpacking District, 22 9th Ave. on West 13th St.
Bill's Marriott Downtown, 85 West St.
www.billsbarandburger.com
This burger joint is still young (2009) but has already sold more than 1.5 million burgers made daily. This feat landed Bill's in CNN's top 10 "Best Burger in America".

THE PERKS OF BEING A CITY GUIDE

Unless my clients are staying well outside the city, I always pick them up at their hotel. So, as a city guide, I've seen my fair share of hotel lobbies. I know the perfect place for a morning coffee, where I can get a good breakfast or, when it rains, an umbrella. At the Langham Place Hotel they take it up a notch: Thanks to their complimentary car service, you are provided with a vehicle. Not just any old racing car, but a Maserati Quattroporte. "So you're asking me if you can take me anywhere in a Maserati? Um, yes please!"

FUN FACT
In case you've already booked your stay at another hotel and would still like to go for a drive in the Quattroporte, you can do so by ordering the homonymous cocktail at the hotel bar. For a mere $176 both cocktail and Maserati will speed you to the highest heights.

52,5%

ENGLISH

23,9%

SPANISH

13,3%

OTHER INDO-EUROPEAN LANGUAGES

7,9%

ASIAN & PACIFIC ISLANDER

2,4%

OTHER LANGUAGES

IMMIGRATION IN NEW YORK

Holland may have been responsible for the founding of New York but, today, only 0.3% of New York's inhabitants are descendants of the Dutch. They are surpassed even by Ukrainians and Hungarians. By far the largest group of New Yorkers have Puerto Rican roots, followed at a safe distance by Italy, the Dominican Republic, China, and Ireland. Surprisingly, in sixth place is not Mexico but Germany, which, in the 19th century, witnessed a great exodus of its sons, in search of farmland and freedom of religion. In 1855 New York had the largest number of German speakers outside of Berlin and Vienna. There was even a Little Germany on the Lower East Side – until the First World War broke out.

102 STORIES

10 MILLION BRICKS

72 ELEVATORS

1,860 STAIRS TO THE OBSERVATION DECK

THE BUILDING'S ZIP CODE IS **10118**

365,000 TONS TOTAL WEIGHT

1,454 FT TO TIP

COMPLETED IN **1931**

20,000 PEOPLE WORK HERE EVERY DAY

CYCLING TOUR

BIKE THE CITY

THE CITY

BIKE THE CITY
THE CITY

🕐 **2 TO 3 HOURS** [MAP I]

1. CENTRAL PARK SIGHTSEEING BIKE RENTAL
2. ABERCROMBIE & FITCH
3. HELMSLEY BUILDING
4. ED KOCH QUEENSBORO BRIDGE
5. ROOSEVELT ISLAND TRAMWAY
6. RAVENSWOOD POWER PLANT
7. ROOSEVELT ISLAND
8. FOUR FREEDOMS PARK
9. EAST RIVER FERRY, HUNTER'S POINT
10. THE UNITED NATIONS
11. EAST RIVER FERRY, MIDTOWN
12. THE WATER CLUB
13. NYU SLEEP DISORDER CENTER
14. NYU COLLEGE OF DENTISTRY

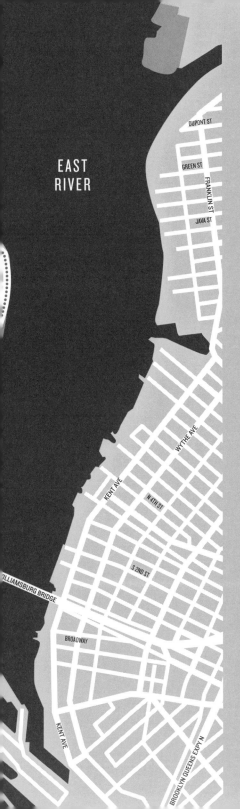

BIKE THE CITY
THE CITY

MAP 2

- ⑮ PETER COOPER VILLAGE / STUYVESANT TOWN
- ⑯ PETITE ABEILLE
- ⑰ ALPHABET CITY
- ⑱ WILLIAMSBURG BRIDGE
- ⑲ MANHATTAN BRIDGE
- ⑳ BROOKLYN BRIDGE
- ㉑ BROOKLYN BRIDGE SIGHTSEEING
- ㉒ SOUTH STREET SEAPORT

Saddle up and pedal your way through fervor, fascination, and fun to fatigued fulfillment. During (and after) this tour you'll have a good view of the east side of Manhattan, the East River and the banks of Queens and Brooklyn. This route could also be taken partially or completely on foot but the route is essentially for biking. There are places along the way to lengthen or shorten the trip depending on your own preferences. Enjoy, but be careful! Before leaving, check the ferry times and your destination's opening hours. This will help everything flow nicely and prevent unpleasant surprises.

❶ CENTRAL PARK SIGHTSEEING BIKE RENTAL

56th St. between 5th and 6th Ave.
www.centralparksightseeing.com
Ready for the New York cyclathon? Before you go overhauling the *Yellow Cabs*, first overhaul your bike. You don't want it costing you an arm and a leg. Be careful: New York traffic is chaotic and comes at you from all directions. Keep an eye out not only for the traffic laws and lights and those biking ahead and around you, but give life the right of way.

❷ ABERCROMBIE & FITCH

720 5th Ave. between 56th and 57th St.
stores.abercrombie.com/ny/newyork
🕐 Mo.-Sa. 10 a.m.-8 p.m.,
Su. noon-8 p.m.
What a dirty duo. A&F is heavily under fire because it spews too much perfume into the air. Certain chemicals are apparently even harmful to the reproduc-tive system. Admittedly, the New York air could use some freshening, but preferably more of the envi-ronmentally friendly kind. Many shoppers turn up their noses at this company and at its discriminatory personnel policy. But it's no biggie for A&F. They even have a client surplus: A&F offered the cast of the MTV series Jersey Shore a pile of money to get them to stop wearing A&F apparel.

❸ HELMSLEY BUILDING

230 Park Ave. on 46th St.
This building served as a railway cathedral and was supposed to elicit oohs and ahs from travelers arriving at Grand Central Station. Now that the trains arrive underground, the building has been deprived of this status, but this created space above ground for more green. And that explains how Park Avenue got its name. The Helmsley Building has the dubious honor of being named after Leona Helmsley, until the end of time. The "Queen of Mean" had an ego to equal the size of the building and drew up a deed stipulating that the building's name would never be changed.

❹ ED KOCH QUEENSBORO BRIDGE

59th St. and 2nd Ave.
Pay attention here. The access path for bikes is actually on 60th Street and 1st Avenue. So you have to ride along the left side of the bridge to 1st Avenue, then make a U-turn to ride up the bridge. It's a steep incline so you'll probably have to stand on the pedals. But your efforts will be immediately rewarded on the other side, where the gentle downward slope of the bridge lets you cruise downhill forever. On your way down, don't forget

to enjoy the phenomenal view of Queens, Roosevelt Island, and the east side of Manhattan.

5 ROOSEVELT ISLAND TRAMWAY

60th St. and 2nd Ave.

If you think the Queensboro Bridge is strictly for pro bikers, there's an alternative with style. The tramwaywill transport you at a height of 250 feet and will take you to Roosevelt Island, bike and all. For the price of a subway ride, you save two bridges and a whole lot of energy.

6 RAVENSWOOD POWER PLANT

Vernon Blvd. and 36th Ave.

If you want to recharge those batteries to be able to push on, then Ravenswood is the right place. This power station supplies power to three million residents. Generator Three, aka Big Allis, was the world's first steam generator capable of producing a million kilowatts. Not too shabby, but today New York consumes 12.5 times as much. The plant also produces steam for direct use. This is the characteristic New York "vapor" you sometimes see escaping out of the manhole covers on the street.

7 ROOSEVELT ISLAND

East River, between Queens and Manhattan

What's in a name? This island between Queens and Manhattan has previously been called Minnehanonck, Varkens Eylandt, Blackwell's Island, Welfare Island, and more. It has been a jail, a smallpox hospital, a mental asylum, and – especially – "inescapable." An ideal spot, therefore, to dispense *personae non gratae*. Now the island is going through a better period. The combination of tranquility, a good view and location make it a much-desired spot for real estate developers and people looking for a place to live.

8 FOUR FREEDOMS PARK

I FDR Four Freedoms Park
www.fdrfourfreedomspark.org
🕐 We.-Mo. 9 a.m.-7 p.m.

At the southernmost point of Roosevelt Island lies Four Freedoms Park, created in honor of President F.D. Roosevelt. New York's newest park refers to the four freedoms in his historic speech, which helped form the United States as we know it today: Freedom of speech, freedom of worship, freedom from want, and freedom from fear. Also, at the en-

trance to this park there is a very hospitable building. The Smallpox Hospital has seen better days but is soon due to be renovated.

9 EAST RIVER FERRY, HUNTER'S POINT

Center Blvd., Long Island City, between Borden Ave. and 54th Ave.
www.eastriverferry.com
Check the website for the ferry times.

Then cast off (your worries). You're not likely to drift off, given the magnificent panorama. The water taxi carries you quickly and safely to the opposite bank for the fair fare of $4 (weekends $6). Your bike can join you for an extra dollar. It can be stowed fore. The terminal is at Midtown, 34th Street. Bon voyage!

10 THE UNITED NATIONS

Between FDR and 1st Ave. and between 42nd and 48th St.
visit.un.org

Probably the most important building in the world. The playhouse features the planet's largest international theater company. Anyone who wants to see a show is advised to follow the world news. The dramas tend to unfold at irregular hours, with the exception of the annual General Assembly in September. During this time, this rigorously secured section of Manhattan is even less accessible. The average entrance fee is an armed conflict, famine, or a tsunami. If your land has oil you get a big discount.

🄫 EAST RIVER FERRY, MIDTOWN

FDR, between 35th and 36th St.
www.eastriverferry.com
Land ahoy! Trade your sea legs for your wheels. In the next stage, you'll cycle towards Lower Manhattan along the East River's west bank.

🄬 THE WATER CLUB

500 E 30th St.
www.thewaterclub.com
🕐 We.-Fr. 5 p.m.-11 p.m., Sa. noon-3 p.m. and 5 p.m.-11 p.m., Sun. noon-3 p.m. and 5 p.m.-10 p.m.
Classic service and decor very much like a yacht club: That's The Water Club's formula. The food is a bit uninspired, albeit neat. And the service is as excellent as the interior is romantic. Definitely ask for a window table.

🄭 NYU SLEEP DISORDER CENTER

27th St. and 1st Ave.
med.nyu.edu
If you've pedaled yourself to exhaustion you can quickly catch forty winks at the New York sleep center. Not surprisingly, The City That Never Sleeps keeps them very busy.

🄮 NYU COLLEGE OF DENTISTRY

345 E 24th St. and 1st Ave.
dental.nyu.edu
One place I've often put my money where my mouth is. Even if your health insurance includes dental, you can still get a bill that'll make your teeth itch. If you can't afford to be picky, the College of Dentistry is a welcome solution. You can have your mouth rearranged here at a reasonable price. Albeit by students and interns. But never look a gift horse...

🄯 PETER COOPER VILLAGE / STUYVESANT TOWN

Lower East Side, between 14th St. and 23rd St. and 1st Ave. and FDR
Peter Cooper Village and Stuyvesant Town are often bracketed together (PCVST) because they're adjacent fashionable quarters. Mr. Stuyvesant was New Amsterdam's last executive director and owned a farm here. Peter Cooper was an inventor and an industrialist who, among other things, built the first American steam train. Well done, boys. Excellent reasons to have a neighborhood named after you.

🄰 PETITE ABEILLE

401 E 20th St. and 1st Ave.
www.petiteabeille.com
🕐 Mo.-Fr. 8 a.m.-11 p.m., Sa.-Su. 9 a.m.-10 p.m.
This is the restaurant I managed during my first years here. It gained me a bunch of new friends and a wealth of information for this book. When in NY do as the Belgians do: Go to Petite Abeille for Belgian fries with mayo or delicious mussels. Just say Patrick sent you.

🄱 ALPHABET CITY

Lower East Side, between 14th and Houston St.
This district has had past lives as a swamp, Little Germany, an immigrant neighborhood, red light district, and drugs quarter. Nowadays, like the rest of Manhattan, it's undergoing gentrification. Since it's on the outskirts, there are more avenues here than on the rest of the island. Negatively numbered avenues would have been confusing and impractical. This was solved by using the alphabet.

⑱ WILLIAMSBURG BRIDGE

The Williamsburg Bridge has been hanging around for more than 110 years between the Lower East Side and trendy Williamsburg in Brooklyn. It may be the least prominent of the BMW trio (Brooklyn, Manhattan, Williamsburg), but this certainly wasn't the case in 1903. Back then it was the longest suspension bridge in our solar system. 111,000 vehicles make the crossing on it every day. In 2012 a handful of them were thrown over the edge by a raging reptile on steroids. Fortunately, Spidey also hangs around regularly.

⑲ MANHATTAN BRIDGE

The Manhattan Bridge alone is worth a bike trip but the view is somewhat obstructed by the fence along the bike lane. The bridge, built in 1909, joins Canal Street: Chinatown's commercial district and *the* place for all things Frucci & Frolex. Although tens of thousands of people use the bridge daily, not until 2014 was it discovered that someone had been living in the support structure between the two levels. Not too expensive and with a fantastic view, but a bridge too far for the authorities.

⑳ BROOKLYN BRIDGE

The Brooklyn Bridge is undoubtedly New York's most famous bridge over troubled water. If you've still got the energy, a jaunt to other side is the perfect extension to this bike tour. The more than a mile-long bridge is toll-free. When it opened in 1883, a crossing cost 5c per cow and 2c per sheep or pig. I'll leave it to you to work out how much that would have cost your whole family. In 1884 a procession of elephants was paraded across it to prove how safe the structure was. A sudden collapse is therefore unlikely but it still pays to keep your eyes open. Tourists aren't too precise about the line between the pedestrian and bike paths.

㉑ BROOKLYN BRIDGE SIGHTSEEING

110 South St., between Beekman St. and Peck Slip
www.brooklynbridgesightseeing.com
⏱ Mo.-Su. 9 a.m.-7 p.m.

All biked out? Time to park your wheels. I hope they turned out all right.

㉒ SOUTH STREET SEAPORT

Pier 17 and thereabouts
www.southstreetseaport.com

Now that your hands are free again, they can grab some shopping bags or a well-deserved milkshake. The area around South Street Seaport is the haven for a fleet of restaurants, food trucks, and shops. One of them is the second Abercrombie & Fitch; just follow your nose. Have fun!

Tia Maria

THE CYCLE OF LIFE

What an angel, my aunt Maria. Born and bred in New York, seventy-something but lively as a spring chicken. She sincerely cares for everyone and gives of herself selflessly.

Her cookies have a name and at Christmas the whole neighborhood is welcome to enjoy her, by now, legendary Christmas celebration. And it isn't a strict traditional ceremony. The bulk of her guests are young and the booze flows abundantly. Once the police even came to stop the party due to the excessive noise.

Tia Maria has had a full life and she's still filling it. Surrounding herself with young people keeps her young, she says. Anyone expecting her apartment's interior to be old-fashioned is in for a surprise. Once I risked asking her why she had never married. She answered "Just lucky, I guess?"

Since she's been living in the city her whole life, Tia Maria is an inexhaustible source of information. I could count on her support for my plans to become a city guide. She really believed in me. My subscriptions to the two most important city magazines, *Time Out New York* and *The New York-*

er Magazine, were a gift from her. To stimulate me further, she also regularly subjected me to pop quizzes about New York City – naturally, with elaborate elucidation when I didn't know the answer.

As befits an inhabitant of this metropolis, she gives her unadulterated opinion about everything. This frequently included comments about my love life: "Patrick, one isn't enough, you need to have several!" And then she would laugh. Since my being married to Ineke, Aunt Maria refrains from passing any further judgment.

As good-natured as she is, one particular subject is guaranteed to get her to fly into a New York rage: Bikers riding on the sidewalk! She doesn't like them. So don't even think about mentioning the Citi-Bike project the city launched several years back. Now, as a result, hundreds of blue city bikes race through the streets. "You can't hear them coming and they just run you over," she states. As a preventive measure nowadays, at her ripe age, she never goes anywhere without her cane. If you ever climb on to a bike in New York be extremely careful. Because of the chaotic traffic *and* because of Tia Maria.

A tip from Tia Maria

KATZ'S DELICATESSEN

205 E Houston St.

www.katzsdelicatessen.com

Katz's has been preparing traditional Jewish food since 1888. It is a real institution whose good name is known far beyond the limits of the Lower East Side and Manhattan. Hundreds of tourists come here every day to taste the famous pastrami and hotdogs. It's still possible to have Katz's send salami to a son or daughter in the army. This tradition began when the three sons from the Katz family were in military service during WWII. Katz's Delicatessen is also where the famous fake orgasm scene from the 1989 movie When Harry Met Sally was shot. I wouldn't go there if you're looking for peace and quiet, but you shouldn't let that hold you back.

RUSS & DAUGHTERS

179 East Houston St.

www.russanddaughters.com

This too is cultural heritage. For four generations, Russ & Daughters have been helping define the city's culinary landscape; from bagels to salmon and caviar. This Jewish family business started out as a food stand and has now been supplying the Lower East Side with delicacies for more than a century.

Biking in New York

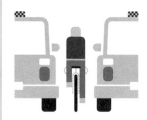

Discovering the city by bike may be gaining in popularity but it's still unadvisable. In most places, at least. The city is definitely making an effort to promote cycling – take the blue Citi Bikes, which are available everywhere – but it still has a long way to go. Even so, the celebrated **Bicycling Magazine ranked New York in its annual top 10 of bike-friendly cities. This is thanks to its ambitious plan to install 1800 miles of bike lanes by 2030. So things are moving. But it will still take some time before New York dethrones Portland, a hipster colony with as many bike bells as djembes.**

Make no mistake: Biking with your family through Midtown is by no means a relaxing day trip. Maneuvering between the sometimes precariously deep potholes, traffic coming from all directions, traffic lights every 100 yards, and not a bike lane in sight: There are better recipes for a good time. Biking in Central Park, however, is marvelous and is also the best way to get to know this

magnificent park. Also the Greenway, the bike trail and footpath surrounding Manhattan, is definitely a good ride. And don't forget the *boroughs*. There too, it's possible to explore New York on scenic, uncrowded paths with, here and there, absolutely spectacular panoramas of the city. The best time for this is in May, when the amazing Five Boro Bike Tour takes you,

FIVE BORO BIKE TOUR
www.bikenewyork.org/
ride/five-boro-bike-tour/

and thousands more bike lovers, through all the New York *boroughs*.

PEDICABS

You couldn't miss them with your eyes closed: Midtown and the Central Park area are swarming with pedicabs, or bike taxis, hoping to tempt tourists into taking a ride. It's not exactly advisable but, if you're determined to be biked around, Central Park would be the place to go. Getting stuck in Midtown traffic is no picnic. Don't flag down your pedicab on the street. Prices can be as high as $5 a minute, while bike rental companies offer a much better deal. If you find yourself in one of the bike taxis anyway, make sure to settle the price and route before the trip. There are hundreds of stories of tourists being cheated out of humongous amounts of money at the end of the ride. And a per-minute price doesn't exactly encourage pedicab drivers to get a move on.

WHERE DO I GET A BIKE?

Citi Bikes are a simple solution for short distances. If you're planning a real bike trip, you're better off with a rental company.

One of the biggest and best organized for bike rentals is Central Park Sightseeing Tours. The bikes are lightweight, reliable, and reasonably priced. Moreover, the company is based only three streets from Central Park. So it's ideal for a verdant voyage. Going into the city anyway? Be extremely careful! It's every man for himself on the road and, unless you're dying to die, the message is watch where you're going. I really mean it!

High water

Water pressure in New York is only high enough to reach the sixth floor. With so many high-rise buildings, this obviously isn't enough. That's why it was decided, in the 19th century, that every building higher than six floors should have a water tower on its roof. A rough estimate assesses the current number of water towers at 10,000 to 20,000. In all their shapes and sizes, they both decorate and deface the New York skyline. New York water, by the way, is of the highest quality, which is an internationally recognized fact. Most of the water is supplied from the more elevated areas in the state's North and West, where it has already undergone natural purification before reaching the city. Whether the water coming out of your faucet is as pure depends to a large extent on the maintenance of the famed water tower on your roof.

FREE SHRIMPS

Bad news for vegetarians. Each mouthful of New York tap water also provides a healthy number of microscopic crustaceans. When it emerged that these copepods were an integral part of the water supply, it caused a brief commotion, especially within the large Orthodox Jewish community who claimed this wasn't kosher. Also, people allergic to crustaceans were anxious for a while. But these tiny creatures are no health hazard. They even help purify the water since they feed on the mosquito larvae that would otherwise contaminate it. In case you're still worried: A simple household filter is sufficient to remove these varmints from your daily dose of city brew.

The five seasons

New York has clearly distinct seasons. The often icy winters and oppressively hot summers mean that spring and fall are the most popular periods for visiting The Big Apple. Footnote: The weather here can be very changeable. Hail, snow, rain, and sun in a single day is not that exceptional. Nor is a 25-degree temperature difference. Besides, each season has its own appeal and its pros and cons.

For the nightlife, you're better off avoiding the summer period. Also, most sports' seasons run from fall to spring. On the other hand, most festivals and open-air events, some of which have free entry, take place in the summer. The sultry weather is just part of the package. Spring regularly surprises you with wet and cold spells, but the sunny moments are very pleasant and New Yorkers enjoy them *en masse* in parks and roof gardens. Generally, autumn is the best time of year. At the end of the fall, the weather can start getting worse, but then the holiday season begins, which happens to be a very fine time to linger in New York. Finally, don't forget that New York has a fifth season, namely the "hurricane season". From the end of May through the end of November, there's always the chance that normal weather forecasts will be turned upside down by the forces of nature. Unless you plan to come in the dead of winter or the height of summer, it wouldn't be unreasonable to be prepared for all weathers.

Why I
never
marri
I got
I gues

got
ed?
ucky,
s.

David

BUREAUS OF FUN

By day, David pumps his creativity into advertising; by night he dreams of original movie scripts. In between he likes to freak out at his own wacky parties or concoct his next Halloween outfit. David is almost never short on inspiration and this is thanks to New York. "All you need is a subway ride to Coney Island! Inspiration comes from life experience. That's why you never travel first class, Patrick. You want that crying baby or that knee digging into your back."

ANGELIKA
FILM CENTER
18 W
Houston St.
www.angelika
filmcenter
.com

New York has a high concentration of advertising agencies, both large and small. The new World Trade Center is intended to be the buzzing epicenter of the advertising industry. David holds his own in this extremely competitive environment. He has launched campaigns for heavyweights such as Mastercard and Microsoft and has recently teamed Steve Aoki with Duran Duran for the introduction of a new Trident chewing gum. Sometimes it can go wrong. An app he was jointly working on, called Bureau of Fun, was developed to fish out the most amusing posts from people's Facebook timelines. I was a guinea pig during the trial stage and immediately found myself confronted with a photo of my recently deceased grandmother. There was still some work to be done...

Advertising may help make ends meet, but David's real passion lies in film. In a city where more than 250 major feature films are screened every year, he sure is in the right place. Being a motion picture freak, he knows all the movie locations. He can show you the place smashed up by Spiderman, where the Ghostbusters subdued their spooks, and where Marilyn's dress rose to fame. He knows all the best places to catch a movie: from the cozy Angelika Film Center in SoHo to the open-air summer screenings in Brooklyn Bridge Park. David also entertains certain ambitions. One of his girlfriends recently collaborated with Quentin Tarantino and brought David into contact with him. I wonder how that turned out.

A tip
from David

FILM FORUM
209 West Houston St. west of 6th Ave.
www.filmforum.org
Film Forum is a small, non-profit cinema with 500 seats and three theaters devoted to independent American movies, foreign art films, and iconic American classics. The atmosphere is pleasant and the prices are reasonable. Definitely worth a visit if you need a break from the major Hollywood blockbusters.

Films in
New York

New York estimates the number of location shooting days in its territory at 30,000-40,000 a year. So there's a good chance you'll stumble upon a few film sets while exploring the city. Curious about what's being filmed? Take a look at the colored NYPD "No Parking" signs, which the film crews post on the street. They always display the name of the movie. Of course, you could always ask one of the crew.

Musea in
New York

New York has more than eighty museums. The American Museum of Natural History and the Metropolitan Museum of Art are two big ones that together could keep you occupied for weeks, if you plan to see everything. And then there are institutions such as the Guggenheim, the Whitney Museum, the Frick Collection, the Cloisters, the Jewish Museum, and many more. The choice is overwhelming and being a guide in these museums should not be underestimated. Below are a few of my favorites, which deserve some extra attention.

MoMA
II W 53rd St.
www.moma.org

The Museum of Modern Art

My favorite museum by far is the MoMA. It's a question of taste, but, if you ask me, the Guggenheim is slightly overrated. The architecture is impressive but it doesn't bring out the best in the art. The MoMa does this much better. When I first moved to New York, it was one of the first museums to which I bought a membership.

MOSEX
233 5th Ave., corner of 27th St.
www.museumofsex.com

If you're not an avid museumgoer, maybe the Museum of Sex will change your mind. Don't expect a museum with audience participation but you will learn everything about sex and sexuality. From its impact on society and the history of pornography to the evolution of prophylactics. The museum also owns an extensive media collection. Before you know it, you'll be a regular museum buff.

TENEMENT MUSEUM
103 Orchard St., Lower East Side
www.tenement.org

The Tenement Museum is an ode to the lives of the many generations of poor immigrants from all over the world who found their way to the Lower East Side in search of a new and better life. It tells the story of a constantly evolving melting pot of faiths, nationalities, and cultures and the countless difficulties this community had to face. A highly interesting museum with a relevance to the city of New York that should not be underestimated.

Bill

LOVE IS BLIND

If you think safely navigating through New York traffic is an adventure in itself, you should try doing it with your eyes closed. Bill was born blind and for him, this is a daily practice. His bus stop was just outside my door and when he would get off I'd help him cross the street. "Hey Patrick, it's so nice to see you!" was always the friendly cry. And then we'd start talking.

Bill's parents found it important for him to grow up normally. He doesn't give much thought to his handicap. But it does demand some adjustment in day-to-day life. Such as seeking assistance when crossing the street. It's "white is walk, red is run" here. Pedestrians don't pay much attention to traffic lights. Neither does Bill.

He is used to strange reactions. Sometimes he gets money from people who mistake him for a beggar. And in the subway a drug addict once burst into tears because he couldn't get his life together, while a blind man seemed to be getting along fine. Usually, Bill holds on to his helper's arm but, once, a woman would only lead him with her voice. She refused to touch him because she was afraid of men. A guide dog would literally be a move in the right direction, but not for Bill. He prefers his cane. You don't have to feed it.

Bill takes it all in his stride. After all, he's had a fulfilling and happy life. On a flight to Israel forty years ago, the girl who helped him cut his steak did the same with his wedding cake. He works as an insurance sales agent and spends his free time playing the piano and singing in a choir. He regularly goes out with his wife, often enough to please just her. A visit to the Empire State Building is pointless to him. But he does enjoy the Circle Line cruises. He feels the wind and follows the guide's descriptions. He also enjoys visiting all the museums that have audio assistance, such as the Museum of Natural History, which he often visited as a child.

Sometimes being blind has its advantages. During the last big blackout, when all of New York was left without power, there happened to be a family party at his home. When the lights went out, he soothed his panicking guests and subsequently led them outside, one by one, down the dark staircase. For once they saw things his way.

One time, his wife Cheryl asked him what he would like to see the most, given the choice. His answer may not have been what she had hoped. "The blue sky" he said, because he'd never seen colors and had no idea what clouds were like.

A tip from Patrick

I love the New York subway but when there's no other choice I take Uber. But be warned: Uber doesn't work like the regular New York taxis. You need an app to use Uber. So don't raise your hand when a car with the Uber logo drives by. And definitely don't get into any old car that isn't a yellow cab that happens to stop when you raise your hand.
www.uber.com

Taxis in New York

The *yellow cab* is probably the most recognizable item on the New York City streets. There are as many as 15,000. Even so, at peak hours, you'll still have trouble getting one. If you need a taxi, just stick out your hand. First, check if the taxi's cab-top number light is on. If it isn't, it means the cab is occupied and all your wild gesticulations won't help. It's a good idea to get into the cab first and, only then, to tell the driver your destination. You have the right, as a client, to be brought to the destination of your choice using the route of your choice. Despite this, many cab drivers will often refuse to go to the less popular destinations. By getting in first, you prevent the freshly conquered cab from leaving you high and dry.

GREEN CABS

Despite their name, the green cabs don't represent the launch of a new eco-friendly era. These are the new *Boro Taxis*. They were specifically introduced to service the outer boroughs, which are habitually ignored by their yellow counterparts. A ride to the outer boroughs often means an empty ride back, which is not exactly cost-effective. For this reason, most of the yellow cabs usually sit tight around the midtown Manhattan area. The *Boro Taxis* are no different from their yellow siblings, except that they are not allowed to pick up rides under East 96th street or West 110th Street or at JFK or LaGuardia Airports.

The Subway

Taking the *subway* is an acquired skill. The following tips could help you find your way.

ROUTE

Underground it's always congested and very often confusing. Make sure you've already mapped out your route aboveground. Can't figure it out? Just pick any New Yorker and ask them. They'll gladly show you the way.

Before diving into the subway, pay attention to the information above the entrance. Some entrances are only for *uptown* or *downtown*. There's often a cross-platform interchange (a passage to the platform where you can take the train in the opposite direction), although that is not always the case.

There are also many smartphone apps to help you navigate the subway. Most stations are equipped with masts, giving you access to real-time information and enabling you to make an emergency call to your city guide, in case you're at the end of your rope.

EXPRESS OR LOCAL

Express trains are very convenient for more remote destinations. They only stop at the main stations and are therefore much faster.

The express trains are depicted on most maps by white circles. The stations where only local trains stop are shown by black ones. The trains also carry signs identifying them as either LCL (local) or EXP (express). So make sure you don't get on an express train if your destination is a local stop. Otherwise, you'll see your stop whizzing by and it'll be a whole lot of stations before you get the chance to locate the platform where you can take the local train back to your starting point. Besides the lost time, you will also experience the emotional consequences, such as shock, confusion, disappointment in yourself, and annoyance.

HOW DO YOU PAY ON THE SUBWAY?

There are two ways to pay on the subway. Per trip or with an *unlimited card*, which provides, you guessed it, unlimited entrance for a specific amount of time. A single ride costs $2.75. *Unlimited cards* are available for one week ($31) or one month ($116.50). The card itself initially costs $1.

Did you know you can load both time and money on to a single card? Only after the unlimited use has expired will your card be charged again. When paying per trip, a single card can be used for up to four persons. An *unlimited card* is non-transferable.

Subway tickets can be purchased at the entrance of just about all stations. The large vending machines accept cash and credit cards. The smaller ones take credit cards only. The machine does not require your PIN, but your ZIP Code. A bit confusing for foreign tourists, but it simply expects you to enter five digits. Have fun with it.

THE LARGEST **CHINESE**
COMMUNITY OUTSIDE OF ASIA

90.000

THE LARGEST **JEWISH**
COMMUNITY OUTSIDE OF ISRAEL

1.500.000

AKA **JEW YORK**

THE LARGEST
PUERTO RICAN
COMMUNITY

723.500

ILLEGAL ALIENS

535.000

44%		WHITE
28%		LATINO
25%		BLACK
12%		ASIAN
0,7%		NATIVE AMERICAN
0,1%		PACIFIC ISLANDER

48%
SPEAK A SECOND
LANGUAGE OTHER
THAN ENGLISH

40%
WERE
BORN
ABROAD

WALKING TOUR

MULTI-ETHNIC TOUR
THE VILLAGES

MULTI-ETHNIC TOUR
THE VILLAGES

🕐 3 TO 4 HOURS

1	ADIDAS
2	CONVERSE
3	PRADA
4	THE MERCER HOTEL
5	THE DUTCH
6	BLUE RIBBON
7	DOMINIQUE ANSEL BAKERY
8	JACK'S WIFE FREDA
9	MOMA DESIGN STORE
10	CHROME INDUSTRIES
11	LE LABO
12	PUBLIC
13	NEW MUSEUM
14	FREEMANS ALLEY AND RESTAURANT
15	RICE TO RICHES
16	LOMBARDI'S PIZZA
17	EPISTROPHY CAFE
18	CHA CHA MATCHA
19	HAPPY BONES
20	MULBERRY STREET BAR
21	GREECOLOGIES
22	DELUXE FOOD MARKET
23	BOWERY SAVINGS BANK
24	ATTABOY
25	LOWER EAST SIDE TENEMENT MUSEUM
26	ECONOMY CANDY
27	ROCKWOOD MUSIC HALL
28	RUSS & DAUGHTERS
29	KATZ'S DELICATESSEN
30	WAFELS & DINGES CAFE

New York has always been an immigrant city. People from all over the world journeyed here in search of a better life. Their customs, traditions, and ideas helped form the most diverse metropolis our society has ever known. It's the world in miniature and that's what makes the city so great. Diversity is the driving force and the uniting element here. It is this diversification that brings you New York at its best. This walking tour takes you from SoHo via NoLIta, Little Italy, China Town, and the Lower East Side to Alphabet City with an array of shops, restaurants, culture, and architecture along the way. Enjoy!

❶ ADIDAS

590 5th Ave.
www.adidas.com
🕑 Mo.-Sa. 10 a.m.-9 p.m.,
Su. 11 a.m.-7 p.m.

Every self-respecting chain store must have a flagship store on 5th avenue. As a major player in sports, Adidas naturally had to follow suit. Although the name is often poked fun at with amusing acronyms, it actually comes from its founder, Adolf (Adi) Dassler. But that shouldn't stop you dreaming about sports all day. Or was it sex?

❷ CONVERSE

560 Broadway, corner of Prince St.
www.converse.com
🕑 Mo.-Fr. 10 a.m.-8 p.m., Sa. 10 a.m.-9 p.m., Su. 11 a.m.-7 p.m.

"Where can I buy some All Stars?" I am constantly bombarded with this question. Well, here! If you like the idea of personalized sneakers and t-shirts,

bring an extra suitcase on your trip.

❸ PRADA

575 Broadway, corner of Prince St.
www.prada.com
🕑 Mo.-Sa. 10 a.m.-7 p.m.,
Th. 10 a.m.-8 p.m., Su. 11 a.m.-6 p.m.

This store's concept is typical of the somewhat decadent image of this devilishly sexy brand. The elegant layout makes it seem more like a museum than a store. If you can allow yourself such a minimalist (read: inefficient) design for such prime real estate, you're probably doing okay.

❹ THE MERCER HOTEL

99 Prince St., corner of Mercer St.
www.mercerhotel.com

This luxury hotel may not be large but it exudes an authentic New York atmosphere. The hectic lobby, just like the rest of the hotel, is graced with an intelligent and elegant

interior. The restaurant is below street level but this doesn't apply to the food. This used to be the offices of the Astor family, one of the richest and most influential of New York's families. Times have changed but the luxury has remained.

❺ THE DUTCH

131 Sullivan St., corner of Prince St.
www.thedutchnyc.com
🕑 Mo.-We. 11:30 a.m.-11 p.m.,
Th.-Fr. 11:30 a.m.-midnight,
Sa. 10 a.m.-midnight, Su. 10 a.m.-11 p.m.

If your date suggests going Dutch, it probably doesn't mean a dinner at this restaurant. Considering the price range, going Dutch at the Dutch may not be such a bad idea. At least then you can avoid "going Greek." The name of this American cuisine restaurant has nothing to do with the Netherlands. They just liked the name.

❻ BLUE RIBBON

97 Sullivan St., between Spring St. and Prince St.

www.blueribbonrestaurants.com

🕐 Mo.-Su. 4 p.m.-4 a.m.

This is where it all started for Blue Ribbon Restaurants. The brothers Bruce and Eric Bromberg got to know their onions in France. Once their education was complete, they whipped up the first Blue Ribbon here. They have been delighting their guests with amazing dishes since 1992. You can taste them until the wee hours without reservations.

❼ DOMINIQUE ANSEL BAKERY

189 Spring Street, SoHo

www.dominiqueansel.com

🕐 Mo.-Sa 8 a.m.-7 p.m., Su. 9 a.m-7 p.m.

You have arrived at the home of the Cronut. This is not a deranged cave dweller, but a croissant-donut hybrid, which causes many enthusiasts to go nuts and broke. If there's no line, you're in luck, or they're sold out. Enjoy your (w)holesome treat!

❽ JACK'S WIFE FREDA

224 Lafayette Street, Manhattan

www.jackswifefreda.com

🕐 Mo.-Sa. 8:30 a.m.-midnight, Su. 8:30 a.m.-10 p.m.

South African/Israeli grandmother cuisine. Jack and Freda are the South African grandparents of the manager, Dean, who moved to the US with his Israeli wife Maya. Yet another colorful New York immigrant story with equally colorful picture-perfect food.

❾ MOMA DESIGN STORE

81 Spring St., between Crosby St. and Broadway

www.momastore.org

🕐 Mo.-Sa. 10 a.m.-8 p.m., Su. 11 a.m.-7 p.m.

Don't spend your entire shopping budget before you've been to the MoMA Design Store. You'll definitely find a gift in this extensive collection of design, art, architecture, and gadgets for the poor chumps who stayed behind.

❿ CHROME INDUSTRIES

238 Mulberry St., between Spring St. and Prince St.

www.chromeindustries.com

🕐 Mo.-Sa. 11 a.m.-8 p.m. Su. noon-7 p.m.

Chrome makes cool, durable, weatherproof bike and moped streetwear and accessories. So even rain-drenched you could still look tough. Military-grade material with a trendy touch. Just what you need to survive the New York streets.

⑪ LE LABO

233 Elisabeth St., between Prince and E Houston St.

www.lelabofragrances.com

🕐 Mo.-Su. 11 a.m.-7 p.m.

This is the ingenious fragrance engineers' lab. They custom brew, mix, and blend your perfume on request. Even the packaging is given a personal touch. But you will have to pay through the nose. With an average price tag of $250, these aromas are strictly for the stinking rich.

⑫ PUBLIC

210 Elisabeth St., between Prince and Spring St.

www.public-nyc.com

🕐 Mo.-Th. 6 p.m.-11 p.m., Fr.-Sa. 6 p.m.-midnight, Su. 6 p.m.-10:30 p.m.

Public offers an industrial decor that emanates a relaxing and romantic atmosphere. The cuisine is classified as free-spirited fusion. Whatever they call it, the food is incredibly delicious and will blow you away. But softly, so as not to blow out the many candles.

⑬ NEW MUSEUM

235 Bowery, between Stanton and
Rivington St.

www.newmuseum.org

🕐 We.-Su. 11a.m.-6 p.m.,
Th. 11 a.m.-9 p.m.

For a change, the New
Museum is not devoted
to famous dead artists.
On the contrary, it tries
to bridge the gap between
the established norms
and contemporary artists
who would rather not be
appreciated posthumously.
It's an incubator for fresh
ideas and a platform for
sharing these ideas with
the world. A neat museum
in an attractively designed
building.

⑭ FREEMANS ALLEY AND RESTAURANT

Freeman Alley, between Bowery and
Chrystie St.

www.freemansrestaurant.com

🕐 Mo.-Th. 11 a.m.- 11:30 p.m.,
Fr. 11 a.m.-11:30 p.m.,
Sa.-Su. 10 a.m.-11:30 p.m.

Usually, I discourage
ventures into dark New
York alleys, but by way of
exception, I recommend a
peek at the far end of this
one. Freemans restaurant
is more or less a restaurant
version of a speakeasy. Behind the small facade, a hip
vibe, fine service, and good
food await you.

⑮ RICE TO RICHES

37 Spring St., between Mulberry St.
and Mott St.

www.ricetoriches.com

🕐 Su.-Th. 11 a.m.-11 p.m.,
Fr.-Sa. 11 a.m.-1 a.m.

In the regular heaven, they
serve rice pudding with a
golden spoon. Six levels
higher, you have a choice of
21. How does Blue Cheese
or Coconut Curry strike
you? To top it off, there's a
whole selection of "Jesus
droppings" (cake, coconut,
cookie, and more crumbs).
Forget the brown sugar.
That's for goody-goody
angels.

⑯ LOMBARDI'S PIZZA

32 Spring St., corner of Mott St.
met Mott St.

www.firstpizza.com

🕐 Su.-Th. 11:30 a.m.-11 p.m.,
Fr.-Sa. 11:30 a.m.-midnight

May I introduce you to the
most ancient pizzeria in the
US (since 1905)? This is as
authentic as it gets. Despite
its advanced age, the pizza is
fresh. Also pricey, no dessert
menu, and cash only.

⑰ EPISTROPHY CAFE

200 Mott St., between Spring and
Kenmare St.

www.epistrophycafe.com

🕐 Mo.-Su. 11 a.m.-midnight

Epistrophy is a simple but
charming Italian bistro with
jumbled furnishing and "la
mama's" food. The homey
atmosphere is emphasized
by groovy jazzy tunes. Live
music every Sunday eve-
ning. Nice and cozy.

⑱ CHA CHA MATCHA

373 Broome Street, Manhattan

www.chachamatcha.com

🕐 Mo.-Th. 8 a.m.-7 p.m.,
Fr. 8 a.m.-8 p.m.; Sa.-Su. 9 a.m.-8 p.m.

Tired? Take a break here!
This enchanting, green
magic potion will give you
at least ten hours of energy.
But with Matcha soft ice,
cake, and affogato on the
menu, you run the risk of a
green overdose.

⑲ HAPPY BONES

394 Broome St.

www.happybonesnyc.com

🕐 Mo.-Fr. 7:30 a.m.-7 p.m.,
Sa.-Su. 8 a.m.-7 p.m.

Coffee made with happy
beans wakes you up even
more. Moreover, ethically
responsible caffeine is
good for a calm heart and it
purifies your conscience.

⑳ MULBERRY STREET BAR

176 Mulberry St., corner of Broome St.

www.mulberrystreetbar.com

🕐 Mo.-Sa. 11 a.m.-4 a.m.,
Su. noon-4 a.m.

This, in the heart of Little
Italy, is one of New York's
oldest bars. The cafe lives

off its glory days as decor for Donnie Brasco, The Godfather, The Sopranos, and many more movies and TV series. But eh, fuhgeddaboudit!

㉑ GREECOLOGIES

379 Broome St., Manhattan
www.greecologies.com
🕐 Mo.-Fr. 8 a.m.-8 p.m.,
Sa.-Su. 9 a.m.-8 p.m.
New York macrobiotic hotspot. Yoghurt in all shapes and sizes from extremely contented cows with guaranteed pasture. Plus, they have never seen one iota of antibiotics. Nice garden for taking a breather from the heat.

㉒ DELUXE FOOD MARKET

79 Elizabeth St., between Grand and Hester St.
🕐 Mo.-Su. 7 a.m.-8:30 p.m.
Hop into this Chinese supermarket for a quick game of "spot the animal." Small hint: Crocodile and frog are possible solutions. Always keep an eye on your dog.

㉓ BOWERY SAVINGS BANK

128-130 Bowery, between Grand and Broome St.
With its classic Roman style, this former head office of the Bowery Savings Bank was the first of its

kind. The solid image was meant to instill belief in the clients that their savings were safe here. This kind of false promise is still being made nowadays but no longer by the Bowery Savings Bank, which has moved. The bombastic room functions these days as a wedding reception venue!

㉔ ATTABOY

134 Eldridge St., between Broome and Delancey St.
🕐 Mo.-Su. 6 p.m.-3:30 a.m.
Attaboy is a small, concealed cocktail bar in the tradition of New York speakeasies. If it isn't 6 o'clock yet, you'll have to come back for one of their masterfully mixed drinks. If you can find the door, that is. ;-)

㉕ LOWER EAST SIDE TENEMENT MUSEUM

103 Orchard St., between Broome and Delancey St.
www.tenement.org
🕐 Fr.-We. 10 a.m.-6:30 p.m.,
Th. 10 a.m.-8:30 p.m.
This museum tells the story of the thousands of immigrants living in tight quarters in the overcrowded Lower East Side tenements. If you want to show your appreciation of the guides

conducting the many original tours, don't be tight with your quarters.

㉖ ECONOMY CANDY

108 Rivington St., between Ludlow and Essex St.
www.economycandy.com
🕐 Mo. 10 a.m.-6 p.m., Tu.-Fr. 9 a.m.-6 p.m., Sa. 10 a.m.-6 p.m.
Economy Candy's impressive stock of sweets is enough to give the entire world population diabetes. If that sounds exaggerated to you, you're probably overestimating the number of people on earth. But seriously, the assortment from home and abroad is simply mind-blowing. I hope you're in the mood for some sticky-sweet nostalgia. Licorice laces, jawbreakers, candy necklaces, and chocolate cigarettes. They've got 'em all.

㉗ ROCKWOOD MUSIC HALL

196 Allan St., between Houston and Stanton St.
www.rockwoodmusichall.com
Every day, starting at 6 p.m., talented artists give it their best shot on one of Rockwood's three stages, often enough for free. Every self-respecting music lover has to go there. And everybody else, too.

❷❽ RUSS & DAUGHTERS

196 Allan St., between Houston and
Stanton St.
www.russanddaughters.com
🕐 Mo.-Fr. 8 a.m.-8 p.m.,
Sa. 9 a.m.-7 p.m., Su. 8 a.m.-5:30 p.m.

Has all that walking made
you a little "hangry"? That's
understandable because
"Oyf a nikhtern mogn ken
men keyn zakh nit fartrogn"
(Everything's unbearable on
an empty stomach). If you
make this statement inside,
they'll gladly serve you. But
don't be surprised if they
want to "schmooze" with
you in Yiddish.

❷❾ KATZ'S DELICATESSEN

205 E Houston St., corner of Ludlow St.
www.katzsdelicatessen.com
🕐 Mo.-We. 8 a.m.-10:45 p.m.,
Th.-Fr. 8 a.m.-noon, Sa. 24/24,
Su. noon-10:45 p.m.

"Send A Salami To Your
Boy In The Army" has
been Katz's slogan since
WWII. That way, during
the difficult moments, he
could seek comfort in a
treat from home. And what
a treat. Don't miss out on
the pastrami. It goes with
anything. Keep the slip they
give you at the door when
you go in. You'll need it to
be let out. Ess gesunt!

❸⓿ WAFELS & DINGES CAFE

Ave. B and 2nd St.
www.wafelsanddinges.com
🕐 Mo.-We. 8 a.m.-11 p.m.,
Th. 8 a.m.-1 a.m., Fr.-Sa. 8 a.m.-2 a.m.,
Su. 8 a.m.-11 p.m.

There's no better way to
end your walk and let the
pleasures of the day sink in
than with a quintessential
Belgian product. I won't
waffle about it: you can have
your waffle and eat it too!

ANDREW

KING OF THE NIGHT

I bumped into Andrew on one of my nightly revels. He's a nightlife consultant for a string of clubs and knows the nightlife inside out. He started at the bottom in a sleazy bar in the East Village, when it was still a very dubious neighborhood. As an assistant, he was working ungodly shifts there until, one evening, a disgruntled customer shot the place to pieces. The bouncer took three bullets and only survived thanks to Andrew's first aid. His decisive actions didn't escape the eye of the owner, who promptly promoted Andrew to the position of manager. He slowly worked his way up from there.

Andrew's stories sometimes seem to be lifted straight from the movies. Once, when he was the manager of the Gansevoort, a cool rooftop bar in Chelsea, one of the clients was a Saudi prince. For a cool $50,000 the latter bought the whole stock of champagne as makeshift water pistols for his swimming pool. Recently, Andrew even said "no, thank you" to Justin Bieber, who was waiting at the door with his entire entourage. Typically New York. Fame and fortune are not enough. If you lack the right profile you just don't get in. Period. On some occasions, absolutely no one gets in. Once, a brand-new, highly elite club turned literally everyone down at the door, for the sole purpose of building an exclusive reputation.

Andrew also taught me the New York *handshake*. This is used to inconspicuously slip some money to a bouncer. You fold the note in such a way that the recipient can quickly see the denomination. Pretty essential for a good first impression. You see, the bouncers are boss and whether or not you get in depends on a multitude of factors. Your chances are best if you arrive early in the evening, looking sharp, surrounded by beautiful women, familiar with nightlife protocol, and prepared to play the game. Once past the bouncers, you face an unobstructed evening. Unless your name happens to be Lindsay Lohan. That one drank herself senseless, went on a rampage, and was gently but firmly escorted outside at Andrew's insistence. Albeit through the back door, in order to avoid the paparazzi.

A FEW TIPS FROM ANDREW

PARTY TIME

USE NAMES
When trying to get in, throw as many names as possible at the bouncer. Your own, in order to build a reputation, and those of your contacts in the club in order to get in more easily.

TO GET DEADED
Means being barred at the door, brushed off.

Never forget to carry an ID at all times. Under-21s are not only prohibited from drinking alcohol, they are usually even refused entrance to bars and clubs. *To be carded* means you've been asked to present an ID. This is the case just about everywhere.

- After 4 a.m. alcohol cannot be served in New York. So set off on your nightly escapades early. However, once the regular bars and clubs have closed, you could always switch to the *afterhours bars*.

- Before this transition, you'd better empty your glass. The open container law prohibits the public possession of cups, glasses, or bottles of alcohol. So cradling your pint outside or downing your own booze on the way to the club is off limits.

- If you want to go clubbing, definitely take Andrew's advice. If you're set on a particular, exclusive joint, come either extra early (before 10 p.m.) or relatively late (after 2 a.m.). Between those hours you can expect a thorough cross-examination.

> ### FUN FACT
> Not to put any ideas into your head, but in New York, both men and women have the right to go topless. This is the result of a lawsuit filed against the city in 1992 by two women, who considered it an act of discrimination that men were allowed to go topless while women were not. The judge ruled for the plaintiffs but it took at least twenty years before it got through to the last police officer – resulting in several major damage claims. Now there is a memo summoning police officers, under no circumstances, to um, bust any topless women. So, ladies, if it really gets that hot: Go for it!

ROOFTOP BARS

THE STANDARD HOTEL
LE BAIN & THE BOOM BOOM ROOM
848 Washington St., between 12th and 13th St.
www.standardhotels.com/high-line

On the top floor of The Standard, you have two options. The Boom Boom Room is a chic cocktail bar implementing a strict dress code and an equally strict entrance policy. If

you're not on the guest list, you'll have to do a convincing song and dance at the door. But the decor definitely justifies the effort, which can also be said of the view. And I'm talking not just about the city, but also about the people. Just across from the Boom Boom Room is the somewhat more agreeable Le Bain bar. It has a charming sunroof and, during the hot summer months, a plunge pool (hence the name). In the winter, the pool serves as an extra dance floor. In case you don't succeed in getting in here either, you could always go to their bathroom. Even that is an experience.

THE GANSEVOORT PARK ROOFTOP
420 Park Ave. S., between 28th and 29th St.
www.gansevoorthotelgroup.com

No guarantee of the presence of spendthrift Saudi princes. Still, even without them, The Gansevoort's roof is nothing to sneeze at. The *loungy* atmosphere draws a varied and decked out crowd and is the ultimate windup to a long day on the town. Or a kickoff, in case the going out is second on the agenda.

230 FIFTH
230 5th Ave. at 28th St.
www.230-fifth.com

On the 21st floor, under a palm tree (or under heat lamps and a blanket in the winter), you can enjoy a view of the glorious Empire State Building, which towers high above this terrace. To be sure of a seat, go early in the evening because it can get pretty hectic

SAFETY FIRST

New York is pretty safe. The crime rate here is even lower than in other parts of the United States. On the list of most dangerous cities, New York ranks around 50th, below cities such as Boston, Chicago, Detroit, Dallas, and Miami. Especially in Manhattan, there's nothing to worry about. You can freely walk the streets or take the subway at all hours of the day. Don't take the Bronx's bad reputation seriously. It's mostly thanks to Hollywood. Naturally, there are some less reputable neighborhoods as well, but that's a given in any megalopolis. Even the Bronx has villa neighborhoods and *million dollar apartments*. Nowadays, whole periods can go by without a single violent death, an enormous improvement on the 2,245 murders in 1990 (an average of six a day).

NIGHT COURT

NIGHT COURT
100 Centre St., Downtown Manhattan
⊙ Daily, 5 p.m.-1 a.m.

If you want to get to know the New York legal system safely and up close, pay a visit to the night court. It was created to help cope with the innumerable arrests the city has to process daily. The sittings are open to the public and are something of an experience. These days, many tourists include a visit to the courthouse on their itinerary. Be well behaved and stay quiet if you don't want to risk a fine or a private inside tour of one of the cells.

STUDIO 54

The legendary nightclub, Studio 54, was well known for its temperamental doormen, who would sometimes refuse entry even to celebrities. As on New Year's Eve 1977 when they sent Nile Rodgers and Bernard Edwards, of disco band Chic fame, packing. The duo wrote a song, that very same evening, with lyrics that began: "Aaaaah, f**k off." But, since they could probably never reach the charts with such words, the next day they changed them to, "Aaaaah, freak out. Le freak, c'est chic." Le Freak became one of the biggest disco hits of all time and the most popular song in the history of Studio 54.

THE COMMERCIAL BLUES

BLUE NOTE

www.bluenote.net/newyork

Blue Note is a monument in the world of jazz music. But what was once a respected institution has evolved into a commercial tourist trap. The music is still first-class but the prices have followed suit. The overly long lines outside are often an omen for the total lack of room inside.

COTTON CLUB

656 125th St.

www.cottonclub-newyork.com

The Cotton Club also has a rich history as a popular nightclub in Harlem. It goes all the way back to those sorry times when only whites were allowed in, at a time when many a major African American artist performed there, helping to create the club's big name. The Cotton Club is not as packed as the Blue Note but, unfortunately, it is following in its footsteps. This club, too, is living off its fame, a fact evidenced by its public as well as by its entrance fee.

MONEY MATTERS

Next to the price of admission, most jazz, comedy, and other clubs also charge a beverage minimum. This means you're expected to order one or two drinks. So don't forget to factor this into your budget.

VILLAGE VANGUARD

178, 7th Ave. South, between Perry and W II St.

www.villagevanguard.com

The decor is nothing to write home about but at the Vanguard they know what jazz is. And that's what you come here for; cozy conversation is not an option. There is no talking or calling during the shows. That would be disrespectful to the sublime music. The entrance fee ($25 - $40) is on the steep side but, considering the quality, worth every cent.

I DEADED
BIEBER A
KICKED C
LINDSAY

JUSTIN
ND
UT
LOHAN.

ANDREW

MR. JAY WHITE

CONCEALED ALCOHOL

This hefty individual is Mr. White. The irony of it needs no further emphasis. I got to know Mr. White when I was in charge of Chinatown's nightlife security. Well, at least that of the Apothéke, an unobtrusive upscale cocktail bar in a forgotten alley, which owes its name, The Bloody Angle, to a sinister mafia past. (The sharp bend in the street made it easy for gangsters to ambush their enemies. As a result, at the beginning of the 20th century, more people had met a violent death there than anywhere else in New York).

The Apothéke is one of the many speakeasies in New York. These concealed bars are a throwback to Prohibition in the 1920s. The production, distribution, and consumption of alcohol were legally banned. But all forbidden things are doubly enjoyable. And profitable. At the time, hard liquor was clandestinely distilled outside the city and sold on the black market. In order to distribute the booze, secret and hidden bars were sprouting like mushrooms. This period is now long gone but its aura of mystery and exclusivity means the appeal of the speakeasy today is stronger than ever. As a consequence, the lines are long. I experienced this the first time I went to discover Apothéke. Fortunately, Mr. White, after studying acting in my home country, had a predilection for everything Belgian. This played to my advantage when he was selecting those worthy of entering from a line of waiting clubbers. Because even though money may open many doors, money alone is not enough here. Everyone has money. "You also need to be somebody." From that point on, I was in Mr. White's good books. Especially his guest books.

A TIP FROM MR. WHITE

JOE'S SHANGHAI
9 Pell St., between Doyers and Bowery
www.joeshanghairestaurants.com
Near Apothéke you'll find Joe's
Shanghai, which serves delicious soup
dumplings on weekdays between
11 a.m. and 11 p.m. A tasty and cheap
alternative to pizza, burgers, or street
meat. It's popular, so come on time.
Otherwise you risk a long wait and/
or having to share a table with other
guests.

SPEAK EASY

New York still has very
many speakeasies. Some
better concealed than
others, but all waiting to
be discovered. But keep
your vacation budget
and remaining brain
cells in mind. Enjoy your
expedition.

APOTHÈKE
9 Doyers St. between Division
and St. James Place
www.apothekenyc.com
Don't be fooled by the sign
(Gold Flower Restaurant)

above the door. This is
where you should be. Inside
are 250 different cocktails
(of about $16) and an
equally tasteful interior. To
your health!

THE BACKROOM
102 Norfolk St., between
Delancey and Rivington
www.backroomnyc.com

You could easily walk past
the Backroom's street
entrance. So keep an eye out
for the iron gate. Go down
the stairs and to the back.
Then through the door and
back up the stairs, open the
door, and walk inside. To
get to the actual *backroom*
you still have to move a
bookcase to one side. This
is one of the last authentic
speakeasies from the 1920s
and, just as it was done back
then, you get your beer in a
brown paper bag and your
liquor in a coffee cup.

PLEASE DON'T TELL
113 Saint Mark's Pl., between
Ave. A and 1st Ave.
www.pdtnyc.com
If you find the hotdog joint
Crif Dogs at this address,
you're in the right place.
Find the phone booth
inside, pick up the horn
and try to get the host's (or
hostess's) attention. With
any luck, you're on your way
to a delicious cocktail. But
please don't tell.

THE GARRET
296 Bleecker St., corner of
Barrow St.
www.garretnyc.com
No secret doors, bells, or
passwords here. Not even
a bouncer maintaining
exclusivity. But to reach the
Garret you do need to go
past the restroomss of the
Five Guys hamburger joint.
Go left, up the stairs, and
you're in your best friend's
apartment. At least that's
how it feels.

RAINES LAW ROOM
48 West 17th St.
www.raineslawroom.com
Hailed by the collective
New York press as one of
the top ten cocktail bars in
the city. Go down the stairs,
push the bell, and hold your
breath. If you're allowed
in, you will be received into
an intimately lit salon with

small, secluded niches to
disappear into.

THE CAMPBELL APARTMENT
15 Vanderbilt Ave.
www.hospitalityholdings.com
In Grand Central Station
there's an elegant cocktail
bar in what was once the
office of businessman
and millionaire John W.
Campbell. For *Gossip Girl*
fans: This is where Serena
and Nate had an interesting
encounter. Be sure to dress
up because if you're in
sneakers and a Hawaiian
shirt, you won't be let in.

INEKE

CLOUD NINE

My New York friends have taught me about the city in many different ways. But the discovery of romantic New York is wholly to Ineke's credit.

My good friend Nigel Williams once honored me with the task of showing his daughter Janice around. I introduced her to New York and she introduced me to her best friend. That was Ineke. A tour for a date? That must be the best deal I've ever made. We arranged to meet on the roof of the elegant and tasteful Americano boutique hotel in the heart of Chelsea. The clouds must have been low that day because, despite being only on the 10th floor, I was on cloud nine. And I wasn't the only one. The attraction was mutual and, before we knew it, we were shuttling between Brussels and New York. Each of Ineke's visits was a fresh opportunity to surprise her. For instance, with the panorama of the mesmerizing Manhattan skyline in Williamsburg, where you could gaze for hours from the water. Or with idyllic spots in Central Park or shopping in SoHo. She couldn't get enough of the view from the Top of the Rock so I gave her an annual pass as a present. We also really enjoy going on explorations by scooter. Riding around unhurriedly, visiting cool stores and checking out new restaurants is a great way to spend the day. The possibilities here are endless and each day is different. And now everybody can follow Ineke's discoveries: Being a genuine New York mom, she started her own blog with daily tips and advice on the best new restaurants, what to go see, and what to discover. The fact that Ineke decided to move to New York because of me makes it, more than ever, "the City of (my) Dreams."

ROMANTIC NEW YORK

LA PISCINE @ THE AMERICANO
518 W 27th St., between 10th and 11th Ave.
www.hotel-americano.com
Ideal rooftop restaurant for meeting the love of your life.

ALICE'S TEA CUP
156 East 64th St. - 102 West 73rd St. - 220 East 81st St.
www.alicesteacup.com
This cute little teahouse is perfect for an elaborate breakfast or afternoon tea and cake. Don't skip the super delicious pancakes. Great for couples and kids.

TARTINERY
209 Mulberry St. or 1 West 59th St. in the Food Plaza
www.tartinery.com
Tartinery has raised the sandwich to an art form. The decor is open and comfortable, the food simple and delectable.

This is a French concept and includes a substantial wine list.

MAGNOLIA BAKERY
401 Bleecker St., corner of W 11th St.
www.magnoliabakery.com
Partly thanks to Sex and the City, this West Village bakery has become immensely popular. Nowadays their cookies, cakes and, of course, cupcakes can be found all over New York as well as far beyond. Beware of the banana pudding! It's deliciously addictive.

STATUE OF LIBERTY

GIFT FROM
FRANCE TO
COMMEMORATE
THE UNITED STATES'
CENTENNIAL

305 FT. HIGH ↕

2 THE COPPER IS
PENNIES THICK
ⓒ ⓒ

THE ORIGINAL
COPPER
COLOR TURNED
GREEN
AFTER 30 YEARS
DUE TO OXIDATION

225 TONS

THE FACE IS
AN EFFIGY OF
THE SCULPTOR'S
MOTHER

THE STATUE
WAS SHIPPED
IN

300

SEGMENTS

UNESCO WORLD
HERITAGE SITE

THE TORCH IS
ACCESSIBLE
BUT OUT OF
BOUNDS

4 MILLION
VISITORS
A YEAR

SWAYS UP TO
3 INCHES
IN THE WIND

THE TORCH
IS COVERED
WITH

24

KARAT
GOLD LEAF

354 STAIRS
TO THE
CROWN

CROWN TICKETS
(TO ACCESS THE CROWN)
BEST TO BOOK MONTHS
IN ADVANCE

Subject index

Photo credits

DESIGN GENIUS

You don't make a book like this on your own. The quest for people with an equal passion for New York brought me to graphic genius Evi Peeters. She has succeeded perfectly in visually portraying this passion. It took Evi months to convince me to use the New York cab yellow. Not only on every page in this book but also for BE NY jackets, bags and gadgets. But she was right: I am now recognized on every street corner as "that crazy yellow guide from Belgium" and Evi's daring design for this book won her a Red Dot Award, the world's most coveted design prize. If you're interested in what amazing stuff Evi is up to now, take a look at evipeeters.be.

'A WAY WITH WORDS'

"So I went to New York City to be born again," the brilliant author Kurt Vonnegut wrote. This applies also to Daan. Just like Vonnegut, as a young writer, journalist, and anthropologist, he stranded on the banks of the Hudson. And those same banks are where, by a favorable twist of fate, I got to know him. Brooklyn is his habitat and Columbia University is his second home. On his literary digital domain, www.daanbauwens.com, he keeps you up to speed on all the multicultural and weird but magnificent things that he could experience nowhere else but here. So you will understand why it was pretty obvious whom I should ask to take care of the American edition of this book.

Acknowledgements

I dedicate this book to my parents, in particular to my mother. Her endless support and infectious optimism were – and are – indispensable to the realization of my dream. Thank you both for the kind and encouraging words in our many phone and video conversations. For the concern, the good advice, and your firm faith in your son. Despite my high school English teacher's prediction that I could only make a career in bobbin lacemaking: Dear English teacher, even without your confidence in my future, I can now inform you that you are mentioned not only in three editions of this book, but also in this English translation. Maybe it could be of some assistance to you as educational material.

Geert, thanks for the shared passion, your talent for writing, your humor, and the many –(wee) hours spent on this book and my business.

Thank you very much, Ineke, for your love and our shared love of New York. Thank you New York, for the unique opportunities.

This book would have been impossible without the support, creativity, and diligence of the following people:

Adam, Adriaan, Alain, Alex, Alexandra, Alice, Andre, Andries, Anja, Ann, Annelies, Anouk, Anthony, Arle, Arno, Arul, Baptist, Ben, Benny, Benoit, Bernadette, Bernard, Bieke, Bob, Bram, Caroline, Cathy, Celine, Charlotte, Chloe, Chris, Christian, Christophe, Claudine, Cor, Daniel, Danny, David, Davy, Delphine, Dieter, Dimitri, Eef, Elke, Emma, Erwin, Esther, Eva, Evert, Evi, Filip, Florence, Frank, Frederica, Frederique, Geertrui, Gerald, Geraldine, Gerard, Gerrit, Goris, Gregory, Griet, Guy, Heidi, Hendrik, Ilona, Ilse, Inge, Iris, Jacques, Janice, Japser, Jean-Marc, Jeannot, Jelle, Jeroen, Jill, Jo, Jos, Joyce, Judy, Karen, Karijn, Kate, Kevin, Kirs, Klaas, Koen, Kristaen, Lars, Laura, Lauren, Lies, Liesbeth, Lisbeth, Luc, Maaike, Mabel, Mandy, Manu, Marc, Margot, Marianne, Mariette, Marion, Mark, Mathias, Mia, Miek, Mieke, Mirese, Miriam, Monique, Morgane, Natasha, Nathalie, Nicolas, Nicole, Nigel, Nikki, Olivier, Patrick, Paul, Pauline, Peggy, Peter, Petra, Philippe, Pierre, Raphael, Remco, Rik, Roderick, Ronny, Roy, Sacha, Samira, Sarah, Serge, So a, So e, Sonja, Stefaan, Stekel, Stephanie, Steven, Stijn, Talita, Tamara, Tanguy, Tanja, Theo, Thibaut, Thomas, Tim, Tom, Toon, Veerle, Veronique, Vicky, Vincent, Wim, Yves.

WITH THANKS TO
Arul, Mildred, Joyce, Bill, Robert, Richard, Seven, Naturale, Jessica, Monica, Tom, Allison, Yvette, Tia Maria, Danny, Shay, Mr. Jay White, Andrew, Bruce, Sean, David, Daniel, Israel, and many, many, many more New Yorkers! New York Magazine, The New York Times, The Wall Street Journal, www.galleristny.com, UJA Federation of New York, JCSNY 2011 Comprehensive Report

BE NY

TAILOR-MADE NY

Do you want to see the city with Patrick van Rosendaal's team too?

BE NY offers many options: From tailor-made private tours to meticulously organized group tours. Feel like a bike ride through Central Park, a cruise among the islands, or a helicopter flight over Manhattan? The sky is literally the limit.

BE NY also organizes business trips and employee perks. Do you want to bond more deeply with your colleagues? We can provide the perfect program. And if your work brings you to New York, BE NY can create the right setting and the right amount of relaxation.

Starting to get itchy feet? Feel free to contact us through the website, www.beny.be or e-mail us at ihavetogotonewyorkrightnow@beny.be

We'll gladly make your stay unforgettable.

TOURS

GROUP TOURS

B2B

WRITTEN BY	Partrick van Rosendaal, Geert Tengrootenhuysen,
	Eva Ceustermans, Daan Bauwens
TRANSLATION	Moshe Gilula
GRAPHIC DESIGN	Duval Branding: Evi Peeters
TYPESETTING	Elke Feusels
COORDINATION	Lannoo Publishers: Anne Haegeman
	Duval Branding: Sofie Hennen, Jana Vervoort
MAPS	Elke Feusels
PHOTOGRAPHY	Robert Caplin et al
COVER PHOTOS	Robert Caplin

WWW.LANNOO.COM
WWW.DUVALBRANDING.COM
WWW.BENY.BE

D/2017/45/386
ISBN 978-94-014-3469-0